The First Book of

Microsoft Excel for the PC

The First Book of

Microsoft Excel for the PC

Christopher Van Buren

SAMS

A Division of Macmillan Computer Publishing

11711 North College, Carmel, Indiana 46032 USA

To my mom,
DONNA HASTIE,
with love.

©1990 by SAMS

FIRST EDITION
FIRST PRINTING—1990

International Standard Book Number: 0-672-27322-5
Library of Congress Catalog Card Number: 90-62053

Acquisitions and Development Editor: *Scott Arant*
Manuscript Editor: *Lisa Bucki*

Production Coordinator: *Steve Noe*
Cover Design: *Held & Diedrich Design*
Illustrator: *T. R. Emrick*
Production Assistance: *Claudia Bell, Jill D. Bomaster,*
Sally Copenhaver, T. R. Emrick, Tami Hughes, Jennifer Matthews,
Cindy Phipps, Dennis Sheehan, MaryBeth Wakefield
Indexer: *Joelyn Gifford*
Technical Reviewer: *Jerry Fisher*

Printed in the United States of America

Contents

vi

viii

ix

Introduction

Acknowledgements

Many thanks, as always, go to my agent Bill Gladstone for keeping my career alive. Thanks also to Scott Arant, acquisitions and development editor at SAMS, for his guidance and to Jeff Palmer for loaning me his printer, which provided fine quality (if slow) output for the drafts of this book. And, of course, thanks to Trudy for all kinds of help and support.

Conventions Used in This Book

As you use this book, you'll notice it includes special typographical elements to highlight the most important information.

Text that you should type in is printed in `special computer type like this`.

Many commands are activated by pressing two or more keys in combination, or selecting a menu and then an option. These keypresses or selections are separated by a dash (-) in the text. For example, Alt-F1 means you should hold the Alt key down and then press F1 (you don't type the dash). A command like File-New means you should open the File menu and select the New option from it.

Q Look for the icon for Quick Steps, which tell you how to perform important tasks in Excel. Quick Steps are listed on the inside front cover of this book.

 Though you can use Excel with both the keyboard and the mouse, look for the mouse icon throughout this book to quickly find mouse instructions.

> ▶ **Tip:** Helpful tips and shortcuts are included in tip boxes throughout this book.

Trademarks

All terms mentioned in this book that are known to be trademarks or service marks are listed below. In addition, terms suspected of being trademarks or service marks have been appropriately capitalized. SAMS cannot attest to the accuracy of this information. Use of a term in this book should not be regarded as affecting the validity of any trademark or service mark.

Microsoft Excel and Microsoft Windows are trademarks of Microsoft Corp. MS-DOS is a registered trademark of Microsoft Corp.

HP DeskJet printer is a trademark of Hewlett-Packard Co.

Lotus 1-2-3 is a registered trademark of Lotus Development Corp.

Chapter 1

An Introduction to Excel

In This Chapter

▶ *A look at the Excel worksheet*
▶ *Excel's database features*
▶ *Excel's charting features*
▶ *Automating Excel with macros*
▶ *Some ideas for using Excel*

This chapter introduces you to Excel's main features. When you purchased Excel, you may have gotten more than you bargained for. Excel offers powerful worksheet features for manipulating numeric information, graphing features for creating many types of charts, database features for simple information management, and special features for automating and customizing the program. The rest of this chapter explains what each of these features provides and suggests some uses for Excel's powerful capabilities.

What Is Excel?

Excel is a spreadsheet program and, like many other spreadsheet programs, it offers three main capabilities. The worksheet features are the primary capability of Excel. Worksheet features let you perform numeric tasks, such as calculating an expense report, balancing your checkbook, or determining if a particular investment is a good one. These tasks operate on numeric information. This book uses the term *worksheet* when referring to worksheet features.

Excel also offers database features. You can perform statistical analysis on data contained in your worksheets, sort large batches of data, find records within a large group and much more.

2

In addition, Excel offers charting features. Charting is the ability to display numeric information in the form of a graph or chart. Graphs and charts are essential for presenting information in a meaningful and memorable way. Excel's charting features do the work for you by converting numeric data to any number of chart types.

The Excel Worksheet

The Excel *worksheet* is an electronic version of a columnar pad. It consists of numerous rows and columns. The intersection of a row and a column is called a cell, the basic unit of any worksheet. All worksheet information is entered into cells. Besides entering information into cells, you can create formulas that automatically add the columns, add the rows, calculate averages, perform statistical analysis and more. By moving to the various cells and entering text, numbers or formulas, you build a worksheet. Some of the worksheets you can build include budgets, income projections, expense projections, travel expenses, checkbook balancing and loan analysis.

The power of a worksheet comes from the formulas you enter into the cells. Formulas automatically calculate information in the worksheet's cells so you don't have to calculate manually. With the on-sheet formulas, you can change the worksheet's data at any time and the formula cells will recalculate new totals based on changes in the data. The worksheet in Figure 1-1 shows an example.

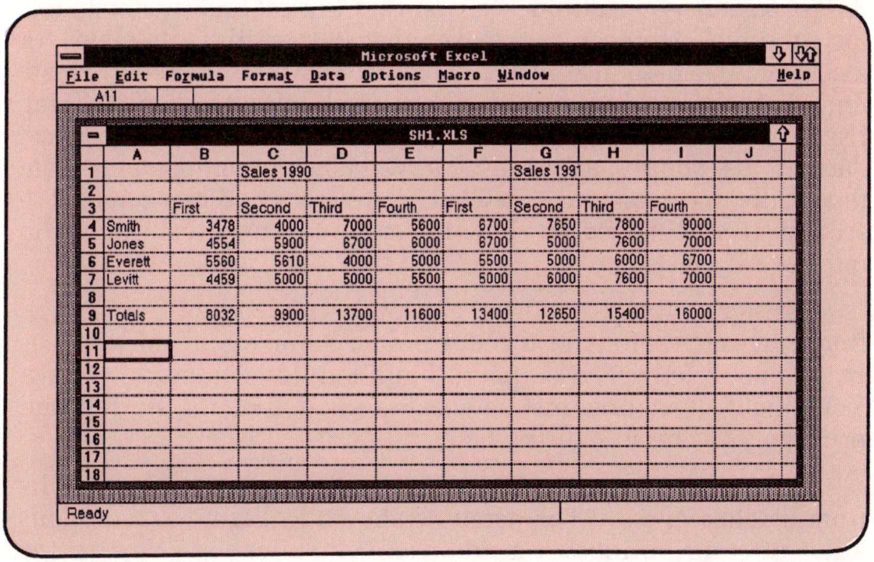

Figure 1-1.   A sample worksheet.

Using a formula, each column of numbers in this worksheet is totalled at the bottom. If you change the values in the columns, the formulas will recalculate the results automatically...and instantly. Using formulas, you could experiment with "what if" scenarios for financial matters. For example, you can compare the amounts of money you would make if you invested your savings over various time periods at various interest rates. Each value you change lets you view an entirely new scenario.

Besides calculating data found in other cells of the worksheet, formulas can access a host of special functions that perform unique operations. One function, for example, computes the average of any group of numbers. Excel offers dozens of special functions.

3

The Excel Database

A *database* is an electronic version of a file cabinet. It stores data for continual reference and makes that data easily accessible. An electronic database also makes it easy to rearrange data and create reports based on information spread throughout the file. Using Excel, you can set up a database within a worksheet. The Excel database is simply an area of a worksheet that contains data repeatedly accessed and extracted for reference. When a database section is established, it inherits extra features that help you retrieve information.

Using an Excel database can be helpful when numeric or financial calculations also require data storage and retrieval, as with general ledger tasks, payroll and employee record keeping. You might even find the database a good tool for storing and printing your basic mailing lists.

Excel databases are also useful for getting statistical results from batches of data. The database shown in Figure 1-2 contains a list of contributions to a non-profit organization. Next to the database is a series of statistical calculations, such as the largest donation, the average donation and so on. Besides getting these statistics on the entire batch of database records, you can calculate these values for subsets of the database. For example, you can find the largest donation within the past six months.

You can set up a database to hold any information you like. Excel provides the tools necessary for analyzing, storing, retrieving and sorting that data. In addition, Excel offers an easy-to-use data *form* that helps you add, remove and find records in the database. The data form that matches the database in Figure 1-2 is shown in Figure 1-3.

Charting with Excel

Charting is the ability to take a table of numbers and represent the data in chart form. Chart types include bar, line, pie and others. Excel's charting capabilities give you total control over each ele-

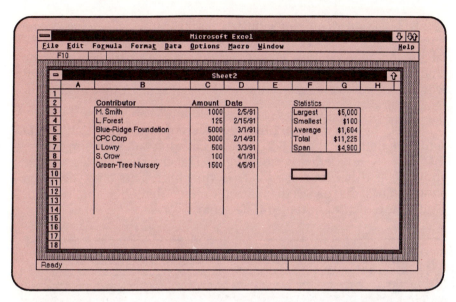

Figure 1-2.   A sample database.

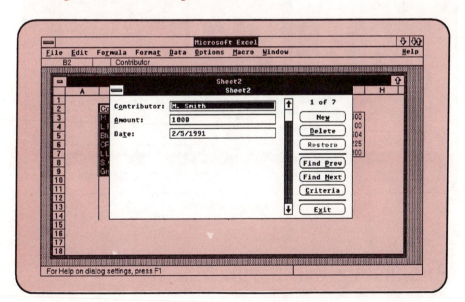

Figure 1-3.   Excel's database data form.

ment of a chart. You can adjust the scale, add titles, change the type of chart, stack the chart, change the printer fonts used for the labels and much more. When the data for a chart changes, the chart adjusts to reflect the changes. Charts are the most powerful way to express numeric data, and Excel's charting capabilities make it easy.

The chart in Figure 1-4 is a basic column chart that represents the data in Figure 1-5. Notice that each sales person is represented by an item in the legend. The quarterly sales figures show up as different sets of bars in the chart. This book's section about charts discusses the various chart elements and demonstrates how you can manipulate them.

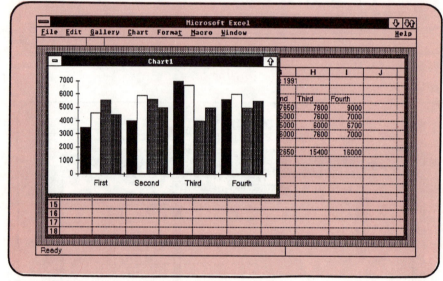

Figure 1-4.   A basic column chart.

Automating Excel with Macros

Macros are little programs that can control any aspect of Excel. Macros are useful for automating worksheet tasks—the same tasks that you might perform manually using basic Excel commands and options. By building a macro, you can perform complex or repetitious tasks with a simple keystroke. This is especially valuable

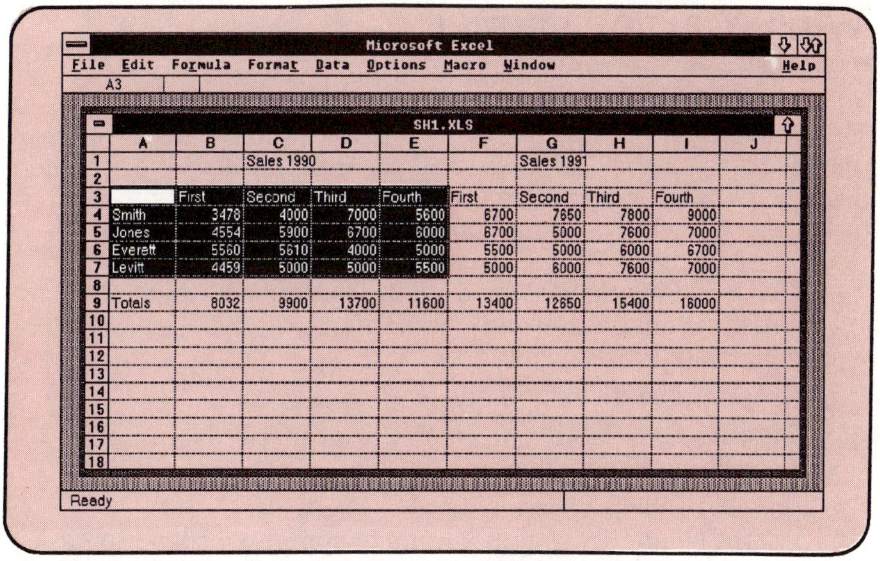

	A	B	C	D	E	F	G	H	I	J
1			Sales 1990				Sales 1991			
2										
3		First	Second	Third	Fourth	First	Second	Third	Fourth	
4	Smith	3478	4000	7000	5600	6700	7850	7800	9000	
5	Jones	4554	5900	6700	6000	6700	5000	7600	7000	
6	Everett	5560	5610	4000	5000	5500	5000	6000	6700	
7	Levitt	4459	5000	5000	5500	5000	6000	7600	7000	
8										
9	Totals	8032	9900	13700	11600	13400	12650	15400	16000	

Figure 1-5. Data used to create the chart.

7

when you build worksheets that will be used by other operators. Macros can control the information entered, check that the information is correct and even control where other operators can move within the worksheet.

Macros consist of a series of macro commands. Like any programming language, macro commands must be combined in specific ways. But macros are simple to create and use. You don't have to know anything about programming to build powerful macros. This book shows you the basics of building macros, providing step-by-step instructions for creating and using them. If you are intimidated by the thought of using macros, don't be. This book makes macros just as simple as any other aspect of Excel. In fact, there are many other aspects of Excel that may challenge you more than macros. So, don't hesitate to jump right into the macro chapters of this book after completing the other chapters.

What You've Learned

This chapter gave you an overview of Excel's three main features: the worksheet, the database and charting. Plus, the chapter described how macros can be used to automate lengthy procedures in Excel. Following are some points to remember:

▶ The Excel worksheet is used to perform mathematical or statistical analysis on numeric data.

▶ The database is used for information that requires repeated access and statistical analysis.

▶ Charting is the ability to represent numeric data in chart or graph form. Excel offers many types of charts and graphs for your worksheet data.

▶ Macros can be created to automate complex or lengthy tasks that you might otherwise perform by hand.

8

Chapter 2

Getting Started with Excel

In This Chapter

▶ *Installing Excel*
▶ *Starting Excel from your hard disk*
▶ *Examining the Excel worksheet*
▶ *How Excel uses your keyboard*
▶ *How Excel uses your mouse*
▶ *Moving around the worksheet*
▶ *Using Excel's menus and options*
▶ *Getting help*
▶ *Quitting Excel*

This chapter gets you started with Excel basics. Before you can really begin creating your own worksheets, you need to know some fundamental things about how Excel works. This chapter includes information about installing and starting Excel; use of menus, the mouse and the keyboard; and some special topics, such as getting help in Excel and using pointer movement commands.

Installing and Starting Excel

The first step in using Excel is to install the program on your hard disk. (As stated on the Excel package, the program requires a hard disk.) If you have already installed Excel, you can skip to the Quick Steps titled Starting Excel.

> ▶ **Note:** If you have a full version of Windows (or Windows 386), it's important that you install Windows first. Then, Excel will be installed under the Windows directory. The installation procedure will help you set up your directories. One advantage to using a full version of Windows is that you can operate Excel with other programs and exchange data between them.

10

If you have not installed Excel, you must do so before continuing. This section shows you how. Note that to use the disks that come in the Excel package, you must have one 1.2M (5.25-inch) floppy disk drive and/or one 720K (3.5-inch) floppy disk drive. If you have only a 360K floppy disk drive, send the fulfillment card provided in the Excel package to Microsoft and exchange the 1.2M disks for the 360K disks. This is inconvenient, but necessary. It means you cannot get started right away. If you are unsure what type of disk drive you have, go ahead and attempt the installation process. It can't hurt to try. If you get the message, Cannot read drive A, when you try to access the installation program, you probably have a 360K drive.

Before you begin the installation process, make a backup copy of your Excel disks, if you have not already done so. Installing Excel is easy. Just start the computer from the hard drive, until the DOS prompt is on the screen. The DOS prompt looks something like this:

`C:\>`

Now insert the disk labeled Setup into your floppy disk drive (this is probably drive A). You can use either the 5.25-inch disk or the 3.5-inch disk, depending on the type of drive you have. Now type

A: SETUP

The screen shown in Figure 2-1 will appear. You are now ready to install Excel. Follow the instructions presented on the screen to complete the process. You will be asked to swap various disks in and out of the A floppy disk drive. When finished, the installation program will have created a special directory on your hard disk for your Excel program, called WINDOWS. You might notice some other additions to your C disk directory, as well.

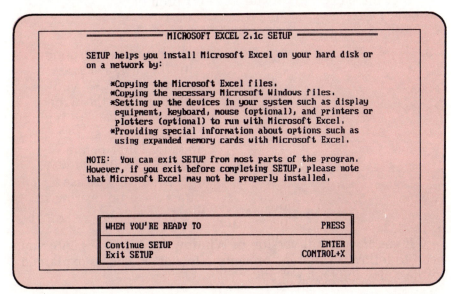

Figure 2-1. Installing Excel.

> ▶ **Note:** During the installation process, you are given the option of using a name other than WINDOWS for storing the Excel program files. This book assumes you accepted the Excel default of WINDOWS.

That's all there is to it. You can now put the floppy disks away in a safe place. Excel is now installed on your hard drive and you can begin using it. To start Excel from the root directory, follow the Quick Steps below.

11

Q **Starting Excel**

1. Start the computer from the hard drive.

   The familiar DOS prompt should appear on the screen. This appears as `C:\>` (or sometimes `C>`).

2. To be sure you have the root directory active, you can type `CD C:\` and press Enter.

   This should take you to the `C:>` prompt.

3. Type `EXCEL` and press Enter.

   If the computer responds with the message `Bad command or file name`, you probably have the wrong directory active. Try typing `C:\WINDOWS\EXCEL` and pressing Enter before typing `EXCEL.` By the way, upper- and lowercase letters have no bearing in this procedure.

12

If you have a full version of Windows or Windows 386, you need to follow a different procedure to start Excel, as explained in the following Quick Steps:

Q **Starting Excel Under Windows or Windows 386**

1. Start the computer from the hard drive.

   The DOS prompt (`C:\>` or `C>`) appears. Some users have an AUTOEXEC file that automatically starts the Windows application as soon as the computer is turned on. If you have such a feature, skip to Step 3.

2. Start Windows by typing `WIN` and pressing Enter. If you have Windows 386, type `WIN386` and press Enter.

   This step begins the Windows environment, where you can see the directories and filenames on the screen.

3. To select the directory that contains the Excel program with the keyboard, press Alt-S to activate the Special menu and choose Change Directory. Type the directory name in the dialog box that appears and press Enter. Using the mouse, simply click on the "\" before the current directory, then type the new directory name in the dialog box that appears and press Enter.

Activates the new directory and displays the files in that directory, including the EXCEL.EXE file.

4. Start Excel from the keyboard by highlighting the EXCEL.EXE file and pressing Enter. Or, simply double-click on the EXCEL.EXE file with the mouse.

Starts Excel.

13

The Excel Worksheet

If everything worked out, you should see the Excel worksheet on the screen. This looks like Figure 2-2.

Using Figure 2-2 as a guide, descriptions of the elements of the Excel screen follow. The names used for the elements will be used throughout the book.

Title bar—The worksheet title bar contains the name of the current worksheet. In Figure 2-2, the title bar shows the name Sheet1. When you open a new worksheet, Excel gives it the name Sheet, followed by a number that indicates how many sheets you've opened this session. Later, you'll see how you can have more than one worksheet open at a time and how the worksheet names play an important role in recognizing which is which.

Control menu
(for program)   Reference area   Title bar   Menu bar   Minimize icon
                 Cancel box   Formula bar   Maximize icon   Restore icon
                     Enter box

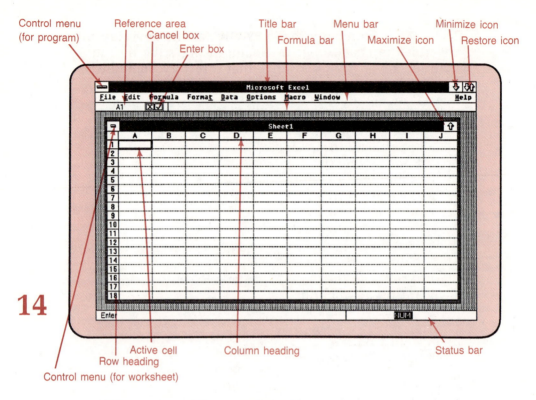

14

Active cell   Column heading   Status bar
Row heading
Control menu (for worksheet)

Figure 2-2.   The Excel worksheet.

Menu bar—The menu bar contains the names of the Excel menus. The menus contain commands and options to manipulate the worksheet. Later in this chapter, you'll get an overview of using menus.

Reference area—This area displays the name of the active cell. See *Cells, the cell pointer and the active cell* below for more details. The name of the active cell is the combination of its column letter and row number. For example, the intersection of column C and row 5 is the cell named C5. This reference is called an address.

Cells, the cell pointer and the active cell—As you know from Chapter 1, a worksheet is made up of cells, which are the intersections of rows and columns. All data is entered into these cells one by one. By activating various cells (one at a time), you can enter data throughout the worksheet. The active cell is highlighted by the cell pointer. You can tell which cell is active in two ways. It is surrounded by the extra thick border and its reference name (address) appears in the reference area. Later, you'll see how to activate any cell you want.

Row and column headings—These headings on the worksheet show you where each row and column is located. As you see in Figure 2-2, rows are numbered and columns are lettered. The intersection of a row and column is a cell.

Status bar—This is a bar across the bottom of the screen that displays information about current settings and the currently selected command (if a command is selected). For example, when the Num Lock, Caps Lock, or Scroll Lock key is pressed, indicators appear in the status bar.

Scroll bars—Scroll bars control which area of the worksheet is in view. They are useful when the worksheet contains too much data to be displayed in a single screen. More details on using scroll bars are included later in Chapter 4.

15

Formula bar and cursor—When you enter information into a cell of the worksheet, it first appears in the formula bar. The cursor indicates the point where information will be inserted when you type. If you like what you have typed, you can accept it to place it in the appropriate worksheet cell.

Enter and cancel boxes—If you have a mouse, you can click on the enter box to accept data you have typed or the cancel box to reject it.

Control menus—These menus contain special commands for controlling windows, such as moving and resizing. See Chapter 4 for more details.

Maximize, minimize and restore icons—These are also controls for manipulating windows. See Chapter 4 for complete details.

How Excel Uses Your Keyboard

The next step is to familiarize yourself with the keyboard and how Excel uses various keys for special purposes. As you use Excel, you will find that many commands and actions can be performed using a number of keyboard methods. If you have a mouse con-nected to your system, you'll have still more ways to accomplish commands and actions. Many people find the mouse the easiest way to control Excel. Others like the keyboard.

Take a look at the keyboard illustrations in Figure 2-3 and find the one that matches yours. Then, review the following information about the various keys and their significance in Excel.

Special Keys

No matter which keyboard you have, there are some keys that deserve special note. Besides the typical alphabet and numerals, keyboards include keys that perform special functions. They are as shown in Table 2-1. When two or more keys are separated by a hyphen in instructions (such as Ctrl-2), it means that the two keys should be pressed at the same time.

16

Table 2-1. *Special Keys*

Key	Function
Enter	(Also known as the Return key.) Accepts an entry or command selection. After typing information, pressing Enter places it into the active cell. After highlighting a menu item, pressing Enter selects the option.
Shift	Creates uppercase letters when used with the alphabet keys. Shift can also be combined with other special keys to create alternative options. You can view special menu options by holding Shift down while you select the menu.
Control (Ctrl)	Invokes Excel's special commands when pressed along with the function keys or other special keys. For example, Ctrl-2 selects a different printer font for the active cell.
Tab	Moves the cell pointer to the next cell.
Direction Arrows ↑ ↓ → ←	Move the cell pointer in the direction of the arrow.
Caps Lock	Invokes uppercase until you press Caps Lock again.

Key	Function
Backspace	Blanks the information in a cell. When the cursor is showing in the formula bar, Backspace erases one character to the left of the cursor.
Delete (Del)	Presents options for clearing the information in a cell or selection. When used with the Shift key (i.e., Shift-Del), Delete moves information to another location on the worksheet.
Num Lock	Changes the numeric keypad into directional keys (see *The Numeric Keypad* below).
Esc	Cancels an action or menu selection.
Scroll Lock	Controls scrolling within a worksheet. With the scroll lock "active," the arrow keys scroll the screen without moving the cell pointer. Pressing the key again deactivates scroll lock.
Pause	Pauses macros.
Function keys (F keys)	Perform special functions. By combining these keys with the Control and/or Shift key, still more functions are available.
/	Activates the Excel menus at the top of the screen. After pressing this key, the next keystroke selects a menu.
Alt	Performs the same function as the / key (above). You can leave the Alt key pressed as you press another key to activate the menu in one smooth action.

17

The Numeric Keypad

The numeric keypad serves two purposes. It acts as a 10-key pad for numeric entry and as directional keys for moving around inside Excel. By pressing the Num Lock key, you can switch between these two basic purposes. When the Num Lock key is active (on), the numeric keypad offers the numbers. When you first start Excel, the number keys are active on the keypad. Therefore, when you press the 2 key, you will get the numeral 2 and not the down arrow (↓) action. Details about moving around in the worksheet are covered under *Moving Around the Worksheet* later in this chapter.

18

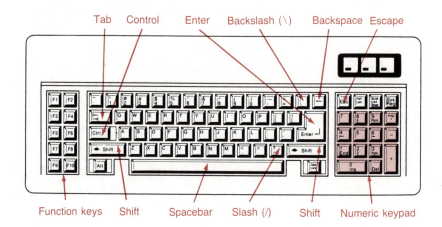

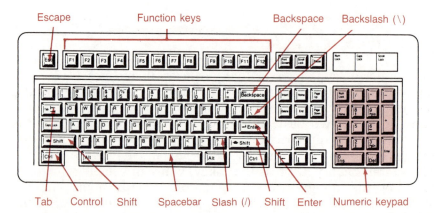

Figure 2-3.   Excel's special keys on each of the PC keyboards.

How Excel Uses Your Mouse

If you are using a mouse with Excel, you will be able to take many shortcuts throughout this book. As you read through descriptions, you'll often notice both keyboard and mouse versions of essential commands and options. The mouse versions are usually the fastest and easiest.

Since mice differ in regard to their buttons, check the manual that came with your mouse for details on the buttons to press or various effects. We will use the following mouse terms:

Click Press the mouse button to select the object or cell on which the mouse pointer is located.

Double-Click Click the mouse button two times in rapid succession. A double-click is often used to open documents from a list. Check your mouse instructions for the proper way to accomplish this action.

19

Drag Press the mouse button and hold it down. Then, move the mouse to another location and release the button. Dragging highlights areas of cells or selects several objects at one time. Again, check your mouse instructions for possible variations in this procedure.

Moving Around the Worksheet

Now that we've gotten some preliminaries out of the way, let's take a look at an important set of commands in Excel: the commands used to move to various parts of the worksheet. As you read earlier, the cell pointer is used to highlight any cell in the worksheet. The highlighted cell is called the active cell. Most of the commands and options in Excel operate on the active cell. Therefore, you need to know how to activate any cell you want.

To move the cell pointer, simply use the four arrow keys on your keyboard. If you use the numeric keypad arrows, be sure that the Num Lock key is not active. The pointer will move one cell in the direction of the arrow each time you tap the key. You can hold down the arrow key for rapid repeat.

To select a cell using the mouse, simply click on the desired cell in the window. The pointer will move to that cell.

Try moving around the worksheet with the arrow keys. You might discover that if you go past the edge of the screen, the worksheet continues and the screen "shifts over" and follows the pointer along its merry way. The worksheet is actually much larger than one screen can possibly display at a time, as illustrated in Figure 2-4.

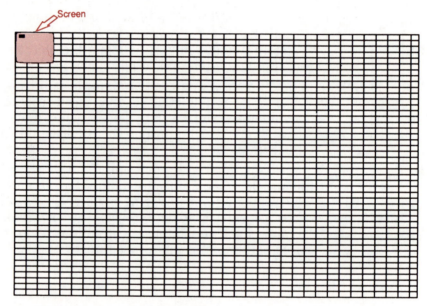

20

Figure 2-4. The worksheet is much larger than one screen can show at a time.

So, you might be wondering just how big this worksheet is. Well, it's 256 columns wide by 16,384 rows long, for a total of 4,194,304 cells! This is more than you will ever need. In fact, if you try to fill up all the cells, you'll probably run out of computer memory before you can finish.

With so many cells, you need a shortcut for moving around the worksheet. If you press the Ctrl key along with each of the four arrow keys, you can move first the corners of the range of cells containing data, then to the four corners of the worksheet as shown in Figure 2-5.

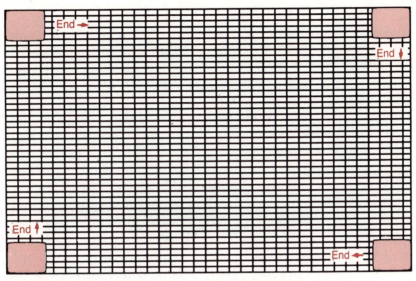

Figure 2-5. *Using the Ctrl key with the arrows to move to the far corners of the worksheet.*

21

At any time, you can move the cell pointer back to cell A1 by pressing Ctrl-Home. Try that now. Cell A1 is always the upper-left corner of the worksheet and is known as the home cell.

A few more movement commands are worth mentioning before we examine the Excel menus. First, pressing the PgUp or PgDn keys move one screen at a time up or down. Pressing Ctrl-PgUp or Ctrl-PgDn moves one screen left or right—farther than the arrow keys but not as far as Ctrl-arrows. You might find these movement commands useful when you create large worksheets.

Finally, let's examine what End and Ctrl-End do. The End key moves the pointer to the last column in the worksheet that contains data, known as the *high column*. Pressing Ctrl-End moves the pointer to the intersection of the last row and column containing data, known as the *high cell*. Follow the example in the Quick Steps below to learn how End and Ctrl-End work.

Q Using End and Ctrl-End

1. Using the pointer movement commands, place the pointer on cell F7.

   Cell F7 is highlighted and the cell address F7 appears in the Reference Area of the worksheet.

2. Type the word SAMPLE and press Enter. (You'll get all the details about entering data in the next chapter.)

3. Press Ctrl-Home to return to cell A1.

   The pointer moves to cell A1.

4. Press End.

   The pointer moves to the high column, in this case column F.

5. Press Ctrl-End.

   The pointer moves to the high cell. In this case, row 7 and column F are the high row and high column. Thus, cell F7 is the high cell. □

22

Table 2-2 summarizes the movement keys for the worksheet.

Table 2-2. *Worksheet Movement Keys*

Key	Moves pointer
↑ ↓ → ←	One cell in the direction of the arrow
Ctrl-↑ Ctrl-↓	
Ctrl-→ Ctrl-←	To the four corners of the worksheet
Ctrl-Home	To cell A1
PgUp PgDn	One screen up or down
Ctrl-PgUp Ctrl-PgDn	One screen left or right
End	To the high column
Ctrl-End	To the high cell
Tab	One cell to the right
Shift-Tab	One cell to the left

Using Excel's Menus

Most of Excel's features and capabilities are controlled by menu options. Excel groups menu options into eight worksheet menus that you see on the screen. The following section provides an overview of the Excel menus. Then, you'll discover how to select options from these menus using either the keyboard or mouse. Details about specific menu options are spread throughout the rest of the book.

Excel offers two ways to view the options in the eight worksheet menus. You can view all options at once, or you can view a subset of the options—just those options you'll need for basic tasks. The shorter version, often used by beginners for simplifying the menus, contains fewer options and is called *short menus*. Excel starts out with *short menus* active.

23

> ► **Tip:** To switch between short and long menus, press Alt, then OM (Options-Menus). Each time you enter the command, Excel will switch between the long and short menus.

File menu—The File menu shown in Figure 2-6 contains options for opening new and existing worksheets, closing the current worksheet, saving worksheets, setting up the print options, printing and print previewing. You can use these commands to create many different worksheets containing unique data. Each worksheet is a separate file which can be manipulated with the File menu's options.

> ► **Tip:** If you close the worksheet using the File-Close command, and if no other worksheets are open, only the File menu and the Help menu remain on the screen. This is because the other seven menus contain options that apply only when a worksheet is active. When no worksheet is active, only the File menu and Help menu options apply. As soon as you open another worksheet, the other menus will reappear.

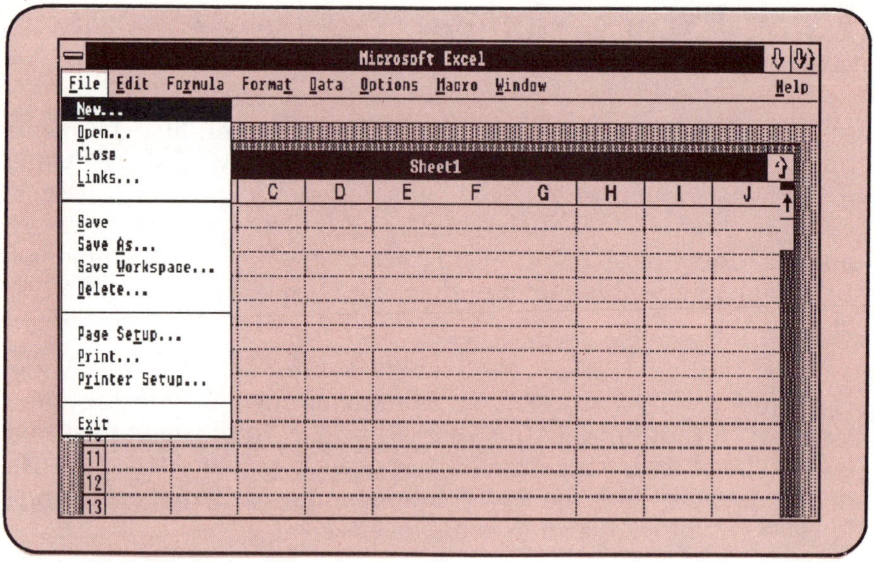

Figure 2-6. The File menu.

24

Edit menu—Options in the Edit menu, shown in Figure 2-7, let you move information within a worksheet or between worksheets, undo errors, insert or delete data, and copy data. You'll find this a frequently used menu.

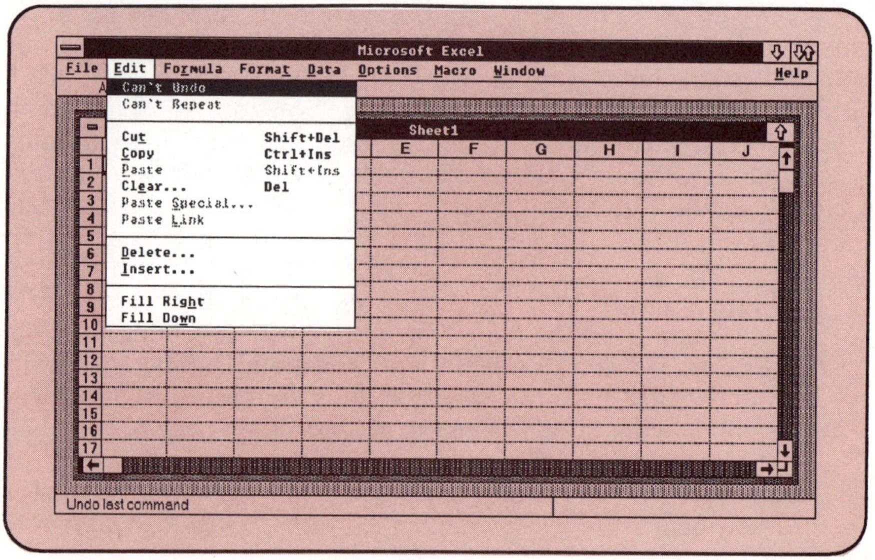

Figure 2-7. The Edit menu.

Formula menu—The Formula menu options are used when you are creating formulas in the worksheet. The options include naming cells, naming ranges and formulas, and finding specific information in cells and formulas. A particularly useful option in this menu is the Note option, which lets you type a special note that applies to a specific cell. This menu is shown in Figure 2-8.

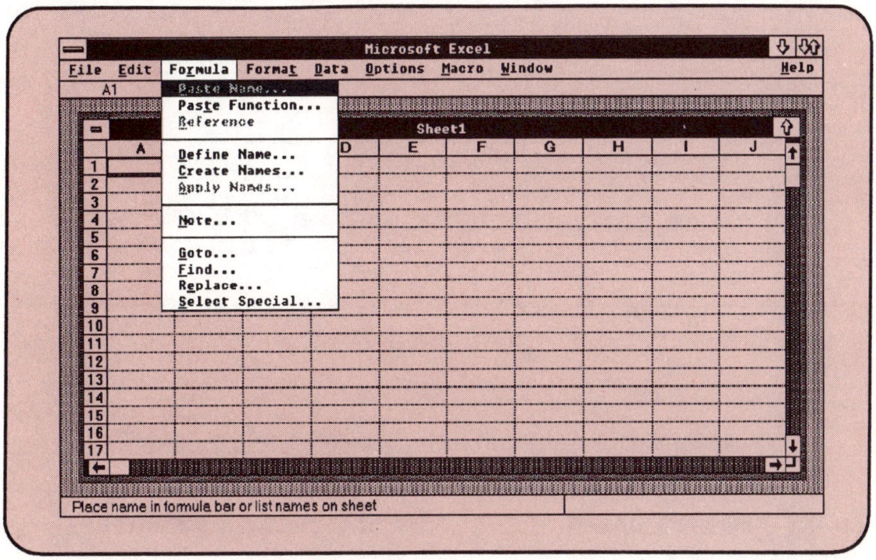

Figure 2-8.   The Formula menu.

25

Format menu—Format menu options help make your worksheets more attractive and readable. You can select printer fonts, sizes and styles for worksheet data; change the appearance of numbers and dates; add borders and boxes around cells; and change the heights of the rows and widths of the columns in the worksheet. The Format menu is shown in Figure 2-9.

Data menu—The commands in the Data menu, shown in Figure 2-10, control Excel's database features. Using these options you can set up a database, search the database for information and extract information. Other options let you sort worksheet information and set up special data tables for advanced worksheets.

Options menu—This menu contains some special options for printing and displaying the worksheet. This menu is shown in Figure 2-11.

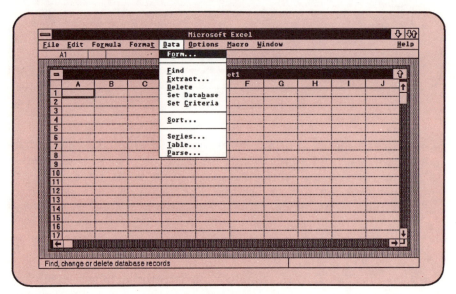

Figure 2-9. The Format menu.

Figure 2-10. The Data menu.

Macro menu—This menu contains options for creating and
running macros. Macros and their purposes are discussed in
Chapter 12. The Macro menu is shown in Figure 2-12.

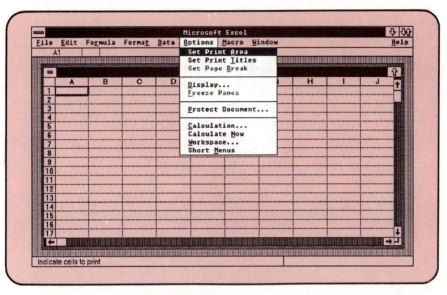

Figure 2-11.   The Options menu.

27

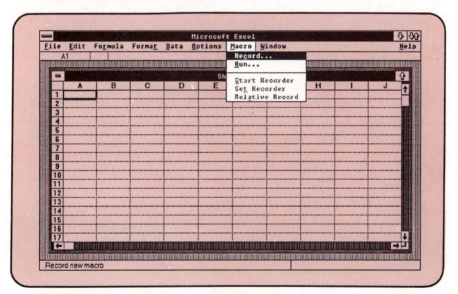

Figure 2-12.   The Macro menu.

Window menu—As you'll discover in Chapter 4, Excel displays each worksheet in a special area, called a window. You can view several windows on the screen at one time and perform special window operations using the options in the Window menu, which is shown in Figure 2-13.

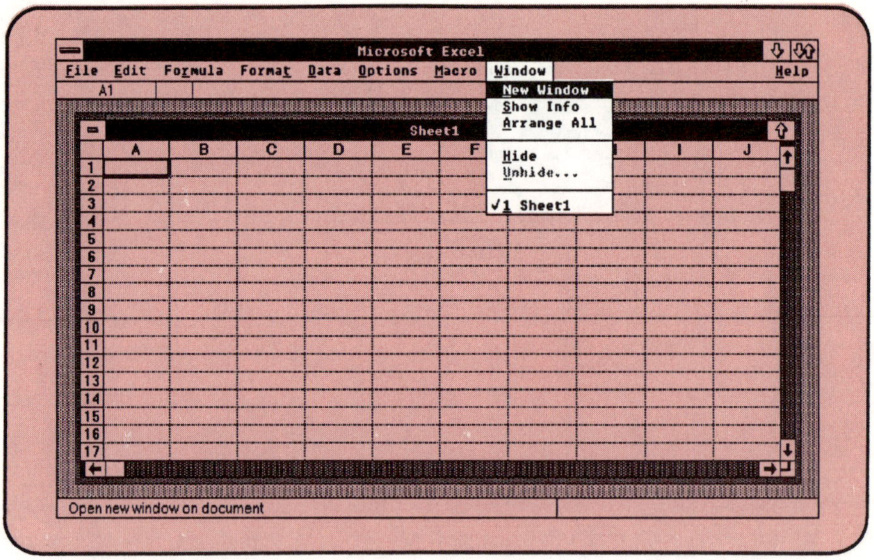

Figure 2-13.   The Window menu.

28

Selecting Options from Menus

You can select menu options using either the keyboard or a mouse. If you have a mouse, you will probably find it the most convenient way to select options. However, read through the following Quick Steps and judge for yourself.

Q Selecting Menus with the Keyboard

1. Press Alt or / (slash), then the underlined letter in the desired menu name. You don't have to release your finger from Alt or the / before pressing the letter of the desired menu.	Activates the menu bar. The desired menu appears, or "pulls down."
2. Press the underlined letter in the desired menu option.	Selects the option within the active menu.

> ▶ **Tip:** You may have noticed that the Alt key performs the same task as the / key. While the Alt key is the normal choice in Excel, the program offers the / key method for Lotus 123 users who are in the habit of invoking menus with this key. You can combine Steps 1 and 2 into a single action by pressing the letter of the desired menu before releasing the Alt key.

Excel offers a second way to use the keyboard with menus. This technique lets you "point" to the menu option you want.

Q Pointing to Menu Options

1. Press Alt or /.	Activates the menu bar.
2. Press → or ← to highlight the desired menu name.	
3. Press Enter.	The menu displays all its options.
4. You can press → or ← again to view other menus.	
5. Use ↑ and ↓ keys to highlight the desired option within the selected menu.	
6. Press Enter.	Selects the highlighted option. □

29

If you use the above technique to view all the menus, you'll notice two special menus at the far left side of the screen. These special menus control the size and shape of the window and are discussed in detail in Chapter 4.

You can actually combine this technique with the previous one for best results. At any time during this process, just press the Esc key to "back out" of any highlighted options and return to the worksheet.

Q Selecting Menus with the Mouse

1. Click the mouse on any of the menu titles. (You can also point to the menu and hold the mouse key down.)

   The options within the selected menu are displayed. The options will remain visible until you choose a command, click outside the menu or press Esc.

2. Click on other menu names. (While still holding the mouse button down, drag across to other menu names on the menu bar.)

   Displays other menus.

30

3. When you find the desired menu, click on the desired menu option or continue to hold the mouse button while you drag down to the desired option and release the button.

   The selected option is highlighted as shown in Figure 2-14 and then invoked.

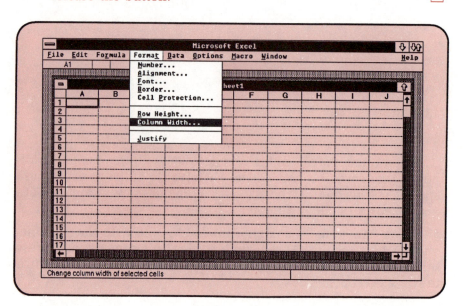

Figure 2-14.   A highlighted menu option.

If you release the mouse button before you highlight a menu option, the menu remains in view. Choose a command, click outside the menu, or press Esc.

> ▶ **Tip:** This book will refer to menu options by identifying the menu name, then the option name. For example, if the book says "Select the File-Exit command," activate the File menu and choose the Exit command within it.

Using Dialog Boxes

Often, menu options produce dialog boxes. A dialog box is a special box that contains options relating to the menu selection. Figure 2-15 shows a typical dialog box.

31

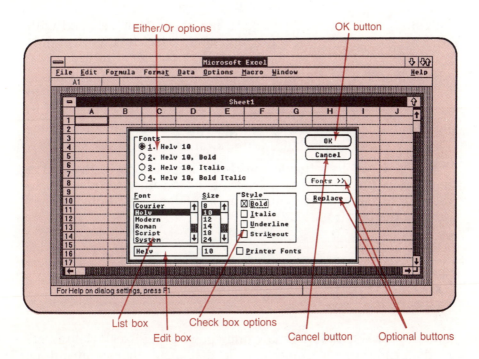

Figure 2-15. A dialog box.

Pressing the Tab key will move from option to option in the dialog box. The currently selected option is surrounded by a dotted line as shown by the "Bold" option in Figure 2-15. When an option is selected, you can often change its setting using an arrow key. You can also select an option by pressing the Alt key plus the letter associated with it (the underlined letter).

 If you have a mouse, simply click on any dialog box option or button to select it. Then click on the OK button.

The following list describes how to manipulate various dialog box elements:

Either/Or Options   After you use the Tab key to highlight one of these options, press the ↑ or ↓ keys to change to a different option. Only one option can be selected at a time.

32   **List Box**   After you use the Tab key to highlight an item in a list box, you can use the ↑ or ↓ keys to change the setting. You can also press the first letter of any item in the list to select it.

Edit Box   This item turns black when selected with the Tab key. After selecting this item, just type the new data you want to use.

Check Boxes   After you use the Tab key to highlight one of these options, press the spacebar to select it and spacebar again to unselect it.

Buttons   After you use the Tab key to highlight a button, press Enter to select it.

When you have made the desired selections in the dialog box, select the OK button to accept those settings. Press Esc to reject the changes you make in a dialog box. Both actions remove the box from view.

Getting Help

You can get help at any time while you're using Excel. Help information can provide important details about the command or option in question. Help topics are listed in the Help menu as shown in Figure 2-16.

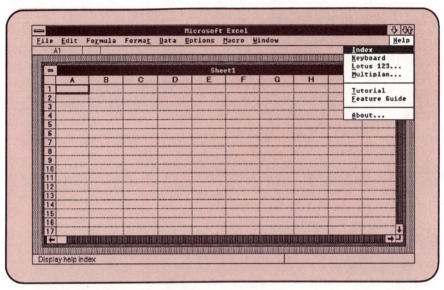

Figure 2-16.   The Help menu.

33

Select the Index option to see a list of topics for which you can get help. Topics are shown in Figure 2-17.

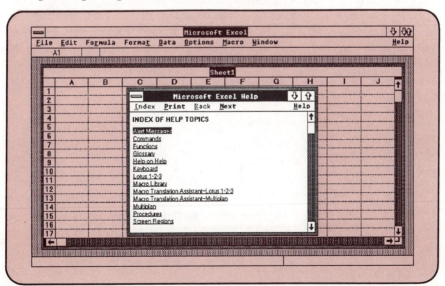

Figure 2-17.   The Help topics.

Enter the first letter of the desired topic or use the ↑ and ↓ keys to highlight it. Then press Enter to view another set of related topics. Now select an item from this second list and press Enter. Finally, you will see the Help screen with useful information. If the information extends past the edge of the Help window, use the PgDn key to move down. Each Help window gives you additional commands as described below:

Index   Press Alt-I to return to the initial index screen.

Print   Press Alt-P to print the current screen.

Back   Press Alt-B to go back to the previous topic or listing.

Next   Press Alt-N to go to the next Help topic or listing.

Help   Press Alt-H to get information on using the Help feature.

Esc   Press Esc to return to the worksheet.

34

Quitting Excel

To quit Excel, use the File-Exit command. Before quitting Excel, be sure to save any data you have created. If you have made changes to existing data, be sure to save the changes. Excel will prompt you to save any worksheets you have changed. Saving worksheets is described in more detail in Chapter 3. At this point, however, you might just want to quit Excel without saving what you have done. The following Quick Steps explain how to quit the Excel program.

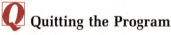 **Quitting the Program**

1. Select the File-Exit command.

If you have not made any changes to the worksheet, Excel will return you to DOS. If you have made changes, Excel will ask, Save changes in ..Sheet1..?

2. Select Yes to save the worksheet or No to throw it out.

3. Enter the desired name for the worksheet and press OK to save it.

If you choose No, Excel returns to DOS. If you select Yes, see step 3.

Excel will return to DOS.

☐

What You've Learned

This chapter provided some of the fundamentals for using Excel. You discovered how to install and start the program and what the various Excel screen elements mean. You also learned how to move around inside the worksheet and how to select menu options. Following are some essential points to remember:

35

▶ Use the Install disk that came with Excel to install the program onto your hard disk. Then, follow the steps that appear on the screen.

▶ Once you install Excel, you can start the program by typing EXCEL at the C:> prompt and then pressing Enter.

▶ If you have trouble starting Excel from the C:> prompt, type C:\WINDOWS\EXCEL and press Enter.

▶ The screen displays only a portion of the entire worksheet at one time. Use the various movement commands to view other parts of the worksheet.

▶ Press Alt or the / key to activate the Excel menus.

▶ Each menu and option in Excel has a letter associated with it. You can type this letter after pressing Alt to select the menu or option.

▶ If you have a mouse, you can select menu options by clicking on the desired menu and dragging the mouse to the desired option, then releasing the button.

▶ You can press Esc to back out of any menu before selecting an option.

▶ Excel offers help at any time. Just use the Help-Index command to display a list of topics.

▶ To quit Excel, select the File-Exit command.

Chapter 3

Creating Excel Worksheets

In This Chapter

▶ *Opening a worksheet*
▶ *Entering data*
▶ *Using formulas and functions*
▶ *Pointing to cell and range references*
▶ *Changing column widths*
▶ *Saving a worksheet*
▶ *Closing a worksheet*

This chapter provides the essential information you'll need to create worksheets. It shows you how to open worksheets, how to enter information into a worksheet, and how to save and close a worksheet. The chapter explains how to enter numbers, text, formulas and dates. After this chapter, you'll be ready to learn about changing existing data in a worksheet and making the worksheet more attractive.

Opening a New Worksheet

You've already seen that Excel presents a new, blank worksheet when you first enter the program from DOS. But you can open another new worksheet at any time. Perhaps you have closed and saved the active worksheet and want to begin a new one. To open a new worksheet, simply select the File-New command from the File menu. The dialog box shown in Figure 3-1 appears.

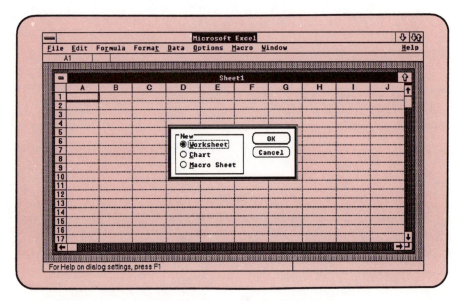

38

Figure 3-1.   Opening a new worksheet.

Excel assumes you want a new worksheet and selects the Worksheet option in the dialog box (as shown in Figure 3-1). Simply press Enter to accept this option and open a new worksheet. You can open a new worksheet even if you have other worksheets currently open. Each new worksheet appears in a separate *window*. (See Chapter 4 for a complete discussion of windows.)

Opening an Existing Worksheet

Once you have saved a worksheet (described later), you probably will need to view it or make changes to it later. You can open an existing worksheet with the File-Open command in the File menu.

The dialog box shown in Figure 3-2 will appear and give you the opportunity to look for existing files in various directories. You can either type the name of the file you want to open, or select it from the dialog box. For example, type

`C:\FILES\EXPENSES`

to open the *EXPENSES* file located in the *FILES* directory of the *C* drive. You can also open a file by selecting its name from the list of available files. To view files in a different directory, select from the list of available directories. When you see the desired file, select its name from the files listing. For information about selecting options in dialog boxes, refer to Chapter 2.

39

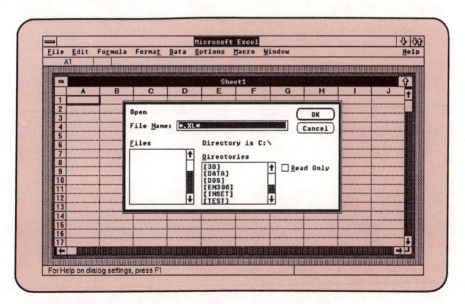

Figure 3-2.   The File-Open dialog box.

Q Opening a Worksheet

1. Select the File-Open command from the File menu.

    The dialog box shown in Figure 3-2 appears.

2. Enter the name of the file you want to open, including any directory path, or select the directory and file from the dialog box listings. Press Enter when finished.

    Opens the worksheet.

□

Entering Data

40

There are four types of data you can enter into an Excel worksheet: *numbers, text, dates and formulas.* These four types of data make up all worksheets.

Number entries are useful for making calculations throughout the worksheet. Excel can "read" the number in a cell and add it to the number in a different cell, for example. Many types of calculations can be performed using numeric entries. A number must begin with a numeral or one of the symbols: + − = . (or $. The period is used as a decimal point for decimal values. Following are some examples of number entries:

1234

$234.23

45%

(35)

−45.89323

If your entry contains alphabetic characters or other symbols, Excel will not consider it a number and you will be unable to use it for numeric calculations. Entries that contain alphabetic characters are considered *text* entries. Text entries are useful for adding labels to your worksheets, such as column and row headings or other descriptive information. Text entries can begin with any character, provided they contain at least one nonnumeric character (such as a letter). Following are some acceptable text entries:

December

ADB − 24

Sixteen

John Smith

Dates are special entries. Excel will recognize the entry as a valid date only if you enter the date in one of the date formats accepted by Excel. If your entries are valid, you can use them to perform *date math*. Date math uses dates in chronological calculations, such as adding a month to a date, calculating a date 30 days from a given date and so on. Using date math requires a valid date entry, as shown in the following examples:

12/1/91

1-Dec-91

12-1-91

41

If you enter a date in any of the above formats, Excel considers the entry a valid date and converts it to a numeric value to perform date math calculations. When an entry is valid, the date will be aligned with the right side of the cell, similar to number entries. You can enter a date in any number of other formats, but if you enter the date in a formula that Excel can't convert to a value, Excel will treat the date as a text entry that cannot be calculated with date math features. Non-valid date entries align with the left sides of the cells, just as any other text entry.

> ▶ **Tip:** Once you enter a date using one of the valid styles, you can change the style. This is described in Chapter 6.

Formulas are special entries that tell Excel how to make calculations based on the values in other cells. Usually, formulas "refer" to other cells containing numeric values. These references are the primary value in worksheets.

Entering Numbers, Text and Dates

To enter numbers, text and dates, move the pointer to the desired cell and type the entry. The entry will appear in the formula bar as you type it. If you are making a numeric entry, be sure that the entry contains only numeric characters or Excel may treat it as a text entry.

Press Enter or use any pointer movement command to accept the entry. If you press Esc before accepting the entry, Excel will not enter the information into the worksheet. If you have a mouse, you can click on the enter box to accept the entry or the cancel box to reject it. When you accept the entry, Excel places it into the cell on the worksheet.

42

If you make a mistake as you type the information, use the Backspace key to back up and correct the entry. If you have already accepted the entire entry, you move back to the cell and retype the entire entry. The new entry will replace the old.

Figure 3-3 shows a worksheet with various numeric and text entries. By pressing an arrow key after each entry, you can move to the next cell and accept the previous entry at the same time. Notice that the numeric entries are aligned with the right side of the cell and the text entries are aligned with the left.

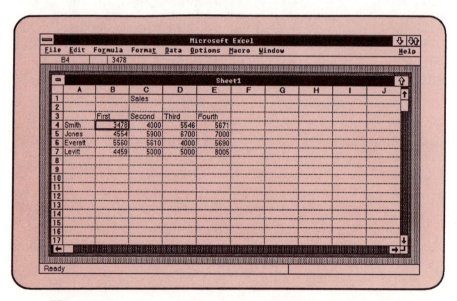

Figure 3-3.   Some numeric and text entries in a sample worksheet.

> ▶ **Tip:** You can change the way Excel aligns numbers, dates and text using the Format-Alignment command. If you don't like the formats shown for dates, but you want to perform date math calculations, you can enter a date in an accepted formats, then reformat the date using the Format-Numbers command. Chapter 6 describes both these commands in more detail.

Entering Formulas

As explained before, formulas calculate the values in other cells of the worksheet. A formula entered into one cell can refer to the contents of other cells by using cell references. (A cell's reference consists of its column letter followed by its row number.) The formula uses references along with mathematical operations to produce calculated results. In general, formulas consist of three elements:

43

▶ An = (equals) sign at the beginning. (An = sign is necessary to create a formula.)

▶ One or more values or cell references that will be calculated. Some examples include:

=**5**	(one constant value)
=**5 + 9**	(two calculated constant values)
=**G12**	(one cell reference)
=**G12 + A2 + 5**	(two calculated references and a constant value)

▶ If you use two or more values (or cell references), you need an operator that defines the type of calculation to be performed, such as addition (+) and subtraction (−).

When you enter formulas, you'll need to use one of the acceptable operators. Table 3-1 shows the operators you can use in Excel for basic mathematical calculations. The following Quick Steps explain how to enter formulas into cells.

Q **Entering a Formula**

1. Move the cell pointer to the desired cell. This cell should be any cell other than those to which the formula will refer. For example, you might enter a formula in cell A3 that adds the values of cells A1 and A2.

   Selects the desired cell.

2. Type the = sign to begin the formula.

   Your entry appears in the formula bar as you type.

3. Follow the = sign with an expression that contains the cell references and an operator.

   At this point, your formula might look like =A1+A2 in the formula bar.

4. Press Enter or use one of the pointer movement keys to accept the entry. Press Esc to reject the entry and start over.

   The entry appears in the cell. If you used Enter to accept the entry, the cell pointer will remain on the cell and the formula will be showing in the formula bar. □

44

Table 3-1. *Operators for Formulas*

Operator	Description	Example
+	Addition	= A1 + A2
−	Subtraction	= A1 − A2
*	Multiplication	= A1*A2
/	Division	= A1/A2
^	Exponentiation	= A1^2

Figure 3-4 shows formulas added to an example worksheet. Notice that the pointer is currently located on a cell containing a formula. This displays the contents of the cell in the formula bar. However, the cell itself displays the *result* of the formula. The beauty of a formula is that you can change the values in the referenced cells, and the formula will automatically recalculate its value based on cell changes.

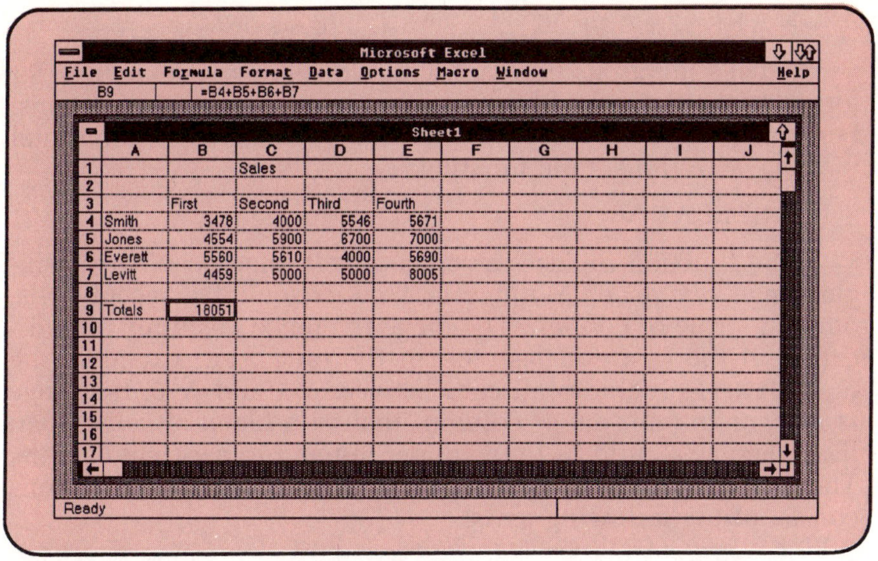

Figure 3-4. Using formulas.

You can stack several expressions together in a single formula if desired. This lets you calculate the values in several cells. An example might read $=A1+A2+A3$. Figure 3-4 also shows this procedure.

▶ **Tip:** Your formulas don't have to use cell references only. You can use constant values in formulas between the operators. For example, you can multiply the value in cell A1 by 5 using this formula: $=A1*5$. You'll get the same result as the formula $=A1*A2$ and entering 5 in cell A2.

45

Using Functions (An Introduction)

You might be thinking about some of the calculations you can perform with formulas. You can use them to add the numbers in a column or to calculate product markups, and so on. But some formulas might be difficult to enter. If you wanted to add the values in a long column, the formula could become rather lengthy:

$$= A1 + A2 + A3 + A4 + A5 + A6 \ldots \text{ and so on}$$

Excel's functions help out. Functions are special entries for formulas that take the place of complex or lengthy calculations. For example, you can replace the previous lengthy column total formula with the simple function:

$$= SUM(A1:A6)$$

The function replaces a series of cell references with a single *range reference*. A *range* is a collection of adjacent cells, often in a row or column. The range reference is simply an indication of the first and last cell in the range. For example, the range A1:A10 includes all cells between A1 and A10. If a range is more than one row or column (that is, a block of cells), then the reference should be to the upper-left and lower-right corners. The reference A1:C3 includes a block of nine cells. All functions consist of the following parts:

▶ The = sign. In the example above, = is entered to make the entry a formula. It is required only when the function appears at the beginning of the entry.
▶ The function name. Each function has a unique name. The example above uses the function named SUM.
▶ The function arguments contained in parentheses. In this case, the argument consists of a range reference.

Keep in mind that each Excel function is unique. Each has a unique name, performs a unique calculation and uses its own requirement for the arguments. A listing of some important functions and more information about cell and range references can be found in Chapter 7 and Appendix A. Figure 3-5 shows the result of several SUM functions.

Pointing to Cell and Range References

Anytime you use a cell reference in a formula or function, you can enter the reference in one of two ways. You can type the reference or point to it. Typing the reference has already been covered. Just type all information in the formula, including the cell references. If you type

=A5

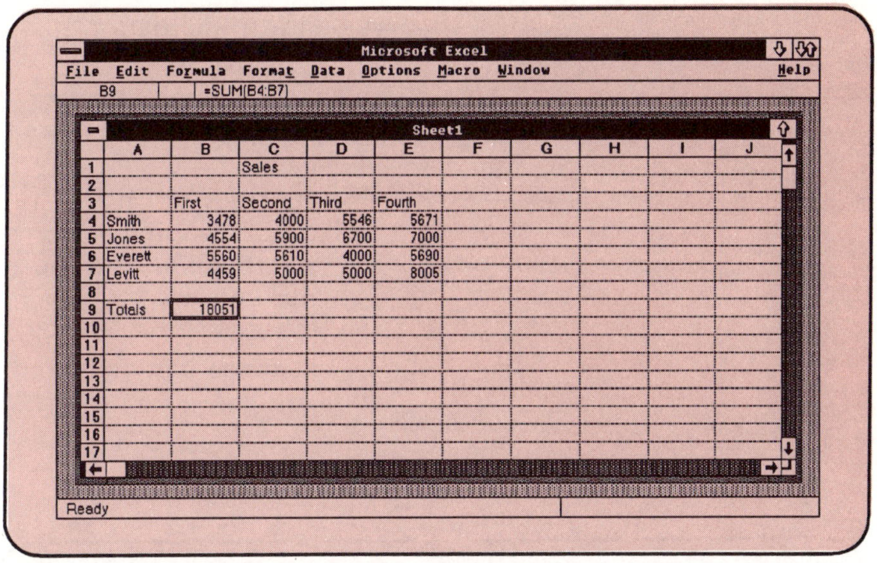

Figure 3-5. Using the SUM function in place of lengthy formulas.

Excel knows that you are referring to cell A5. How does it know this? Because you have begun the entry with the = sign, Excel knows that the cell is not going to contain text. Hence, the A5 must be a cell reference and not a text entry.

However, anytime you are ready to type a cell reference, you can, instead, point to the cell using the arrow keys as the following Quick Steps explain.

Q Pointing to a Cell

1. Enter all elements of the formula up to the reference, including the = sign and any functions.

   Your entry appears in the formula bar.

2. Use the arrow keys to move to the cell you are referencing.

   When you use the arrow keys while Excel is expecting a cell reference, Excel enters "Point" mode. The word Point appears on the status line at the bottom of the screen and a

3. Enter the + sign or any other operator.

The marquee returns to the active cell awaiting your next point action, and the operator appears next to the previous cell reference.

dotted cell highlight (called the *marquee*) will reflect the cell to which you are pointing. Figure 3-6 shows an example.

4. Use the arrow keys again to point to the next cell.

The marquee highlights the cell.

5. Press Enter to complete the formula.

48

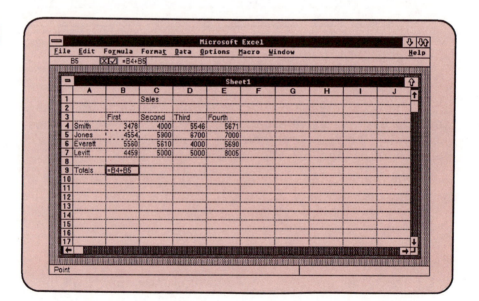

Figure 3-6.   Using the ↑ to point to a cell while entering a formula.

Pointing to a cell with the mouse is as simple as clicking on the cell that you want to use in the formula. Be sure that you have started the formula by typing the = sign, then point.

Remember, you can use the pointing action any time you would normally type a cell reference. When using functions like SUM that require a range reference, you can also point. To point to a range reference, first enter this much of the function:

```
=SUM(
```

Next, point to the upper-left cell of the range, then hold the Shift key down while you move to the lower-right corner using the arrow keys. The marquee will stretch to encompass the entire range. Press) (right parenthesis), then Enter when finished.

Changing Column Widths

49

The *column width* is the number of fixed-pitch characters that will fit into a column. Thus, if the column width is eight and the cell is formatted in Courier (a fixed-pitch type), eight characters will fit into the cell. However, if you format the cell in Helvetica with a column width of eight, more than eight characters will fit into the cell.

As you enter data into a column's cells, you might find that an entry exceeds the width of its cell. This is often the case with text entries. When the cell immediately to the right of an "over-stuffed" cell is empty, Excel allows the entry to spill over to the adjacent cell. Figure 3-7 shows an example.

Note that the entry is not split between the two cells. It is contained entirely in the original cell (cell A8 in Figure 3-7). The contents of cell A8 are simply allowed to appear in cell B8. However, if cell B8 contains an entry, the contents of A8 will not cover up that data. Instead, Excel will display as much of the information as possible. Figure 3-8 shows an example.

When your data entries are too wide for a column, you might want to change the column width so it displays the entire entry. You can change a column's width using the Format-Column Width command, as illustrated by the following Quick Steps.

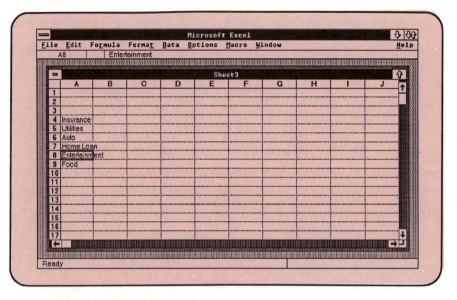

Figure 3-7. *When a cell's entry does not fit into the cell, it will cover up the adjacent cell, provided the adjacent cell is blank.*

50

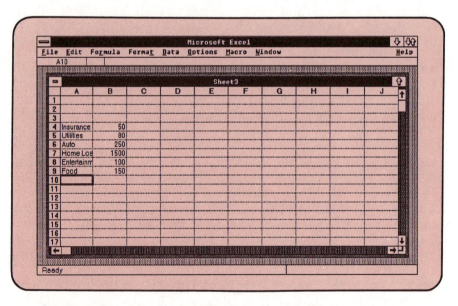

Figure 3-8. *If an adjacent cell contains information, entries to the left will not spill over into that cell.*

Q Changing a Column's Width

1. Place the pointer in any cell in the column that you want to change.

2. Select the Format-Column Width command.

   Excel presents a dialog box.

3. Type the desired column width into the space provided.

   This may replace the width currently being displayed.

4. Press Enter to accept the change or Esc to reject it.

   The column width changes. □

To change a column's width using the mouse, move the mouse pointer to the row heading area at the top of the column. Now move the pointer to the line dividing the column you want to widen and the column to the right. Click on the line and drag to the right to expand the column, or to the left to shrink it.

51

Figure 3-9 shows the column from Figure 3-8, now widened for the information previously too wide to fit into the column.

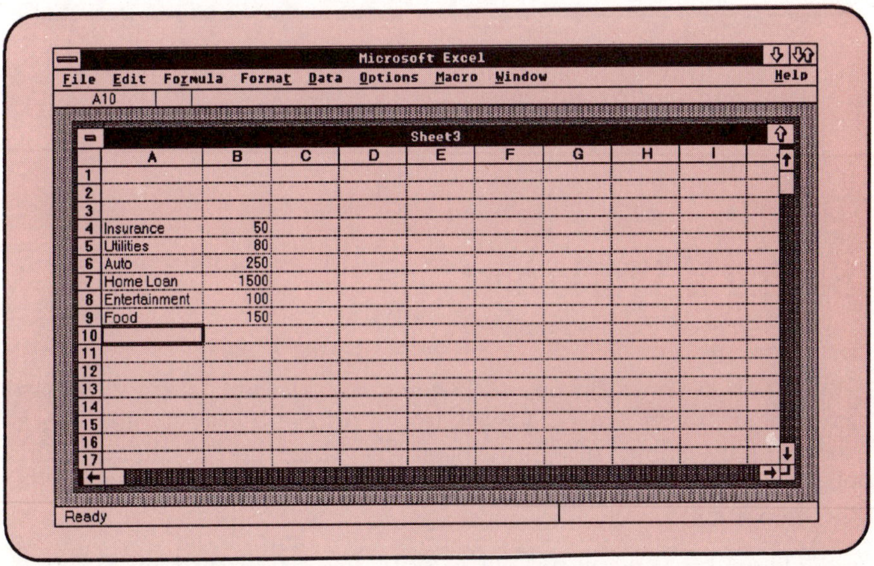

Figure 3-9. Changing a column's width using the Format-Column Width command.

You can change the widths of all columns at one time by pressing Shift-Ctrl-Space and then using the Format-Column Width command. Pressing Shift-Ctrl-Space highlights the entire worksheet as shown in Figure 3-10.

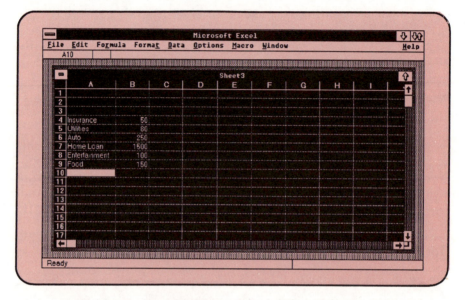

Figure 3-10. Highlighting the entire worksheet for column-width changes.

Saving a Worksheet

When you begin building worksheets, you'll want to know how to save them to save yourself work in the future. If you create a worksheet using some of the procedures described earlier in this chapter, you can save your experiments at any time using the File-Save command.

The first time you save a worksheet, you will be asked to enter a name as shown in Figure 3-11. The name can be up to eight characters long and must begin with a letter. You should avoid using spaces in worksheet names. If you type a period in the name, you can then type a three-character extension. Including an extension, the name can be up to 11 characters long. If you do not include an extension, Excel adds one for you. This extension appears as .XLS. Unless you have a reason for doing so, avoid using extensions and let Excel apply them for you.

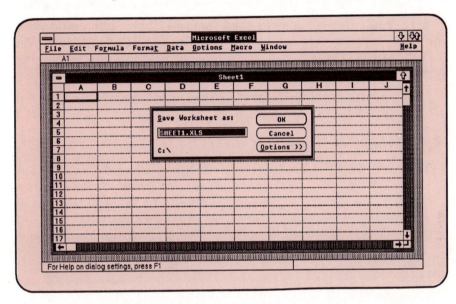

Figure 3-11. Saving a new worksheet requires that you give the worksheet a name.

When you enter a name for the worksheet, you can specify a DOS path name if desired. The path name consists of the disk name and any directory names preceding the worksheet name. If you specify a path name, Excel will store the worksheet in the specified directory. For example, if you type

C:\BUSINESS\EXPENSES

Excel stores the file under the name *EXPENSES.XLS* in the *BUSINESS* directory on the *C* drive. Of course, the specified directory must exist first. If you don't specify a directory path, Excel stores the file in the default directory. The default directory is displayed at the bottom of the Save dialog box as you can see in Figure 3-11. Often, this will be the C:\WINDOWS directory. If you want to store the file in the default directory, just type a name and press Enter.

53

> ▶ **Tip:** For details about creating directories and using directory paths, refer to a book about DOS basics.

If you've saved a worksheet before, Excel will update the old file with any changes you've made since the last time you saved. The worksheet will be stored on disk and will remain in view on the screen. You will not be asked to name the file.

You can save a worksheet using the following Quick Steps.

Q **Saving Your Worksheet**

1. Select the File-Save command.

   Excel will update and save a worksheet you've saved before or ask you to enter a worksheet name.

2. Type any name you like for the worksheet. The name can be up to eight characters long and should not contain spaces. Excel will automatically add the .XLS extension for you. Press Enter or S to save.

   Excel saves the worksheet, and it remains on the screen.

There may be times when you want to save a file under a new name, even though you've saved it under a different name before. This technique is useful for making a copy of the file. Both copies of the file will be stored on disk. Saving a worksheet under a new name requires only a simple variation on the File-Save procedure. Just select the command File-Save As instead of File-Save. Then you can enter a name for the new file.

> ▶ **Tip:** It's a good idea to periodically save your work with the File-Save command. In case of a power failure or other catastrophe, a recent copy of the file will be stored on disk. Of course, you should also make backup copies on floppy diskettes from time to time.

Closing a Worksheet

Saving a worksheet does not remove it from the screen. This requires closing the worksheet. Whether you've saved a worksheet or not, you can close it using the File-Close command. If the worksheet does not require saving, it will be removed from the screen. If you have made changes to the worksheet, you will be asked if you want to save the worksheet before closing. You can opt to save the changes or not. Either way, the worksheet will be removed from the screen. (You can press Esc at this point to return to the worksheet, canceling the File-Close command.)

Closing a worksheet does not exit Excel. After closing all worksheets, Excel displays only the File menu and the Help menu on the screen, since no other menu is necessary. To quit Excel, use the File-Exit command.

55

What You've Learned

This chapter has provided the essentials for starting worksheets. You now know how to enter data into a worksheet, save the data and use it again later. You can begin to experiment with various formulas that calculate the data stored in other cells of the worksheet. Remember, when you change the data in the referenced cells, the formulas will recalculate and present new values. Following are some important points:

- ▶ The File-New command begins a new worksheet.
- ▶ To re-use a previously saved worksheet, use the File-Open command and specify the name of the desired file. Include the entire directory path.
- ▶ Excel distinguishes between four types of data: text, numbers, dates and formulas. Formulas usually calculate the numbers found in other cells.
- ▶ Formulas must begin with an = sign and contain cell references and operators.
- ▶ Excel's worksheet functions perform special calculations and can often be used in place of complex formulas.

▶ You can type cell and range references or point to them whenever you would normally type them.

▶ Use the Format-Column Width command to change the widths of columns throughout the worksheet.

▶ Use the File-Save command to save a new or existing worksheet. If the worksheet already exists on disk, Excel will replace the old copy with the new one.

▶ To change a worksheet's name while saving, use the File-Save As command.

▶ The File-Close command removes a worksheet from the screen.

56

Using Windows

In This Chapter

This chapter provides details about using windows in Excel. In Excel, each worksheet you create exists in its own window on the screen. You can change the size and shape of this window and move it to other locations on the screen. By opening several windows at one time and then changing their sizes, you can effectively view two or more worksheet areas at once. Windows can contain either different worksheets or parts of the same worksheet. This chapter provides details about the usefulness of windows.

Shrinking and Expanding Windows

When you plan to have multiple windows in view, you'll probably want to shrink one or more of them. Changing window sizes helps you get all the information in view. Not only can you shrink each and every worksheet window, but you can change the proportions at the same time or expand the window later. The following sections show you how to shrink or expand windows.

Excel provides a convenient way to manipulate windows using the keyboard and menu options. Following are the Quick Steps:

Q Changing Window Size with the Keyboard

1. Press the Alt key. — Invokes the menu bar.

2. Press the - (dash) key. You can also press the ← key. — Selects the worksheet's Control menu. The screen should look like Figure 4-1.

3. Press S for the Size option. — A four-sided arrow icon appears in the middle of the worksheet as shown in Figure 4-2. This icon tells you that Excel is waiting for you to choose one of the four sides of the window.

58

4. Press any of the four arrow keys. — The arrow key you select tells Excel which side of the window you want to move in. If you press ↓, you'll be able to move the bottom of the window up; if you press ←, you'll be able to move the left side of the window inward; and so on.

5. If you selected the top or bottom of the window in the previous step, press either ← or → to select one of the corners of the worksheet. If you selected the left or right side of the window in the previous step, press either ↑ or ↓. — Selects one of the corners. Figure 4-3 shows an example of moving to the lower-right corner by pressing ↓, then →.

6. Press any of the four arrow keys to manipulate the corner of the worksheet.

Shrinks or expands the worksheet. Figure 4-4 shows what the worksheet looks like when you shrink it from the bottom-right corner.

Figure 4-5 shows the resulting worksheet.

7. When you are satisfied with the size of the window, press Enter to accept the changes you've made, or Esc to reject them.

□

59

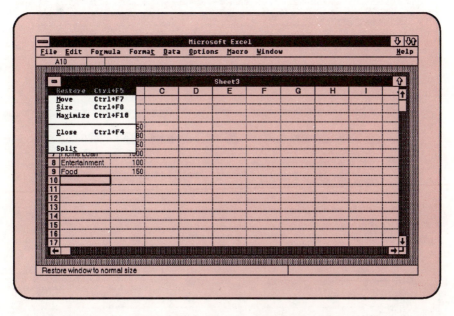

Figure 4-1.   The worksheet's Control menu.

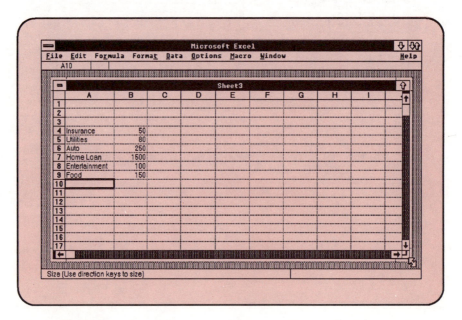

Figure 4-2.   The direction arrow icon.

Figure 4-3.   Getting to a corner of the worksheet
window.

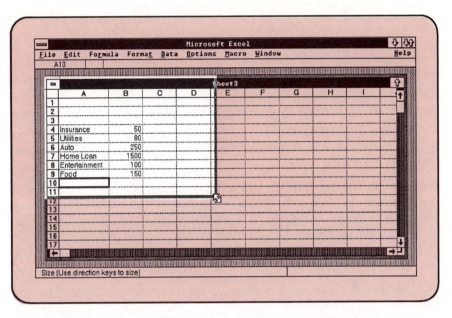

Figure 4-4. *Shrinking a window from the bottom-right corner.*

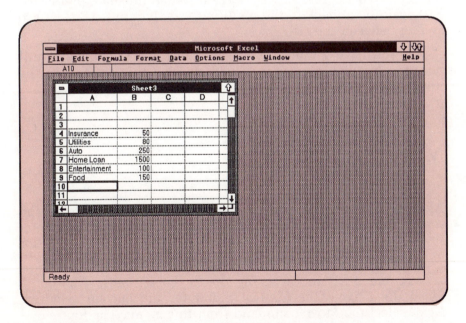

Figure 4-5. *The result of shrinking a window.*

> ▶ **Tip:** You can avoid the first three steps by simply pressing the shortcut key Ctrl-F8. Hold the Ctrl key and tap the F8 key. This brings you to the stage shown in Figure 4-2.

At any time, you can resize the window by repeating these steps.

If you have a mouse, the easiest way to shrink a window is to simply move the mouse pointer to the bottom-right corner of the window, press the button and hold it down. Then, drag the mouse up and to the left to shrink the window. Release the button when finished. Figure 4-4 shows an example of using the mouse to manipulate the bottom-right corner of the window.

62

After you shrink a window, you can easily return to the original, full-screen size by using the Maximize command in the worksheet Control menu. You can invoke this command with the keyboard or mouse. But a faster way to return a window to its full size is to press Ctrl-F10. Try it. When finished, press Ctrl-F10 again to go back to the modified size. Just press Ctrl-F10 to switch between the two sizes.

If you have a mouse, you can return a window to its full size by clicking on the Maximize icon that appears in the upper-right corner of the worksheet.

Moving a Window

After you shrink a window, you can move it to another area of the screen. Moving windows enables you to organize the screen when several windows are open. Keyboard and mouse instructions for moving windows follow.

To move a window using the keyboard, press Alt then - (dash) to activate the Control menu for the current window. Next, select the Move command from this menu. The four-sided arrow appears in the title bar of the window, indicating that Excel is ready to move the window in any direction. Press any of the arrow keys to move the window. When finished, press Enter. To move a different window, activate the window then repeat the process described above.

It's easy to move a window using the mouse. Simply move the mouse pointer over the window's title bar (the top of the window containing the name), press the mouse button and hold it down. Next, drag to another location on the screen and release the mouse.

Using Multiple Windows

Now that you're familiar with shrinking, expanding and moving windows, try opening more than one at a time. This is where resizing a window comes in most handy. Why would you want to open two or more windows at the same time? Well, you might have two separate worksheets that contain related information. While using one worksheet, you might need to view the information in another. Having them both open and in view makes this possible.

63

Opening a Second Worksheet Window

To view several worksheets at one time, open each worksheet using the File-Open command. Just because one worksheet is already open does not mean that you can't use the command again to open another. Simply specify the name of the second worksheet when Excel asks for the name of the file to open. (The File-Open command was discussed in detail in the previous chapter.)

When the new worksheet window comes to the screen, it will appear on top of all other open windows as shown in Figure 4-6. Figure 4-6 also shows that the second worksheet window has been shrunk using the various resizing commands.

Keep in mind that you can only work on the worksheet that is on top of the others. This is called the active worksheet. If the windows are small enough, the active worksheet might not actually appear on top of the others, but beside them. Nevertheless, only one worksheet is active at a time. If you are ever in doubt as

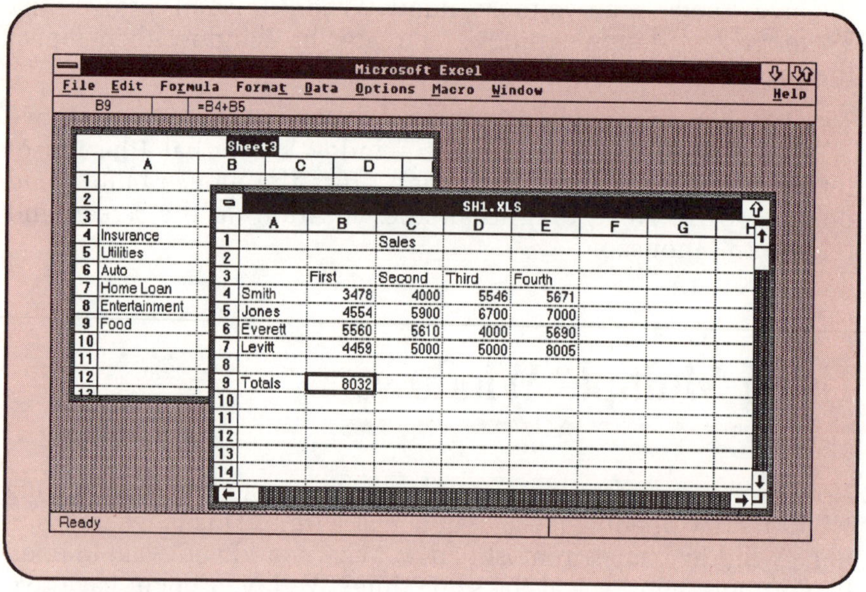

Figure 4-6. Two open worksheets, one of them active at a time.

to the active worksheet, just compare the title bars in the open windows. The active worksheet's title bar is completely black. In addition, you can see the scroll bars on the active worksheet but not on an inactive worksheet.

If you open an additional worksheet, before it's resized it might fill the entire screen and cover up all other windows. That's fine. You can still switch between the various open worksheet windows as described in the next section or shrink the window to a more manageable size.

Switching Between Open Windows

The easiest way to switch between windows is to press Ctrl-F6. This command moves to the next open window on the screen. Keep pressing Ctrl-F6 to switch from window to window. Use Ctrl-Shift-F6 to move backward through windows (when you have more than two). If you have numerous windows open, you can move to a particular one by selecting its name from the Window menu. Just press Alt-W to see the window menu options and find the desired name at the bottom. Highlight the name and press Enter. Alternatively, you can use the mouse to select the desired name from the Window menu. Figure 4-7 shows an example of the Window menu with several windows open. Notice that the active window has a check mark beside its name. This is another way to determine which window is currently active.

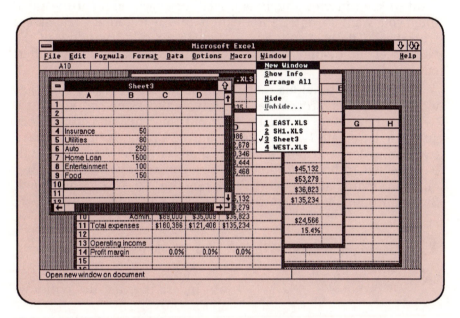

Figure 4-7.   The Window menu showing several window names.

65

Putting Windows Away

You might have already guessed how to put a window away. Just activate the window you want to remove and use the File-Close command as described in Chapter 3. If you have made changes to the worksheet, Excel will ask if you want to save those changes before closing the worksheet.

Two Windows of the Same Worksheet

Rather than viewing two different worksheets at the same time, you might need to view two parts of a single worksheet at the same time. Suppose you have a large block of information that you want to keep in view, such as a table or chart, while at the same time you want to enter information into a different area of the worksheet. The best solution is to open a second window of the worksheet and display various parts of the worksheet in the different windows.

Unlike the previous discussion about viewing two different worksheets, this procedure shows you the same worksheet in two separate windows. Keep in mind that this procedure does not actually create two copies of the worksheet. It only displays two copies for your convenience. Changes to the worksheet will be reflected in both windows. When you remove the windows, only one copy of the worksheet remains on disk. The Quick Steps for opening a second window of a worksheet follow.

66

 Opening a Second Window of a Worksheet

1. Activate the desired worksheet.	The title bar turns black, indicating that the window is active.
2. Select the Window-New Window command.	Duplicates the active window, providing two identical views of the same worksheet. ☐

The next time you look at the Window menu, Excel displays the names of the two windows at the bottom of the menu. Excel has added :1 to the original window worksheet name and :2 to the new window as shown in Figure 4-8.

When you first create a new window, it will appear full-sized on the screen. You may want to change the size of the two windows for convenience. To close the worksheet, you must close all the windows associated with it.

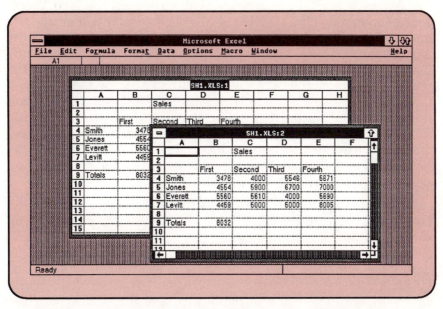

Figure 4-8. Two windows of the same worksheet.

Saving Window Arrangements

The final discussion in this chapter is about saving your window arrangements. If you resize a window manually (using the Control menu or the mouse rather than the maximize icon) or open multiple windows of the same worksheet, Excel will remember the arrangement when you open the worksheet the next time, provided you save your worksheet by using the File-Save command. When you open the worksheet the next time, it will appear with the same window arrangement it had when you saved it.

That procedure's great for individual worksheets, but you can also save the window arrangements when you have more than one worksheet on the screen at the same time. In other words, when you open several different worksheets and then arrange their windows on the screen, you can save the arrangement for future use—even though the windows belong to separate worksheets. You can then easily return to all the worksheets in their saved arrangement.

To save a window arrangement, use the File-Save Workspace command. This tells Excel to save a special workspace file on the disk. This workspace file lets you go back into all the worksheets and their arrangements as you left them. After using the File-Save Workspace command, Excel asks you to name the workspace file. Enter a name with the .XLW extension (you might have to replace the default name of RESUME.XLW). Excel then saves the file on disk. Note that this new workspace file does not replace the files for the individual worksheets that were open. It is used in addition to the original files. Also, saving the workspace file does not save the worksheets themselves. You should save the worksheets individually.

To go back to the workspace arrangement, use the File-Open command and enter the name of the workspace file you saved (including the extension). The related files and window arrangements appear on the screen. In addition to saving the workspace file after you make any changes to the worksheets, you might be asked to save changes to one or more of the worksheets that are open. It's important to save the worksheet files, because saving the workspace file only saves changes to the window arrangements, not changes to the different worksheets.

68

What You've Learned

This chapter discussed the various window capabilities of Excel. Excel's window powers come from the special environment, called Windows, which can be used for many different programs. With Excel, however, you don't need to purchase Windows separately. You get many of the convenient window features free. Following are some points to remember:

▶ To shrink or expand a window, press Ctrl-F8, then one of the arrow keys. This selects one of the four corners of the window. Next, use the arrow keys to shrink and expand the sides of the window. Press Enter when finished.

▶ If you are using a mouse, change a window's size and shape by dragging the lower-right corner of the window.

▶ Pressing Ctrl-F10 returns a window to its full size. Pressing Ctrl-F10 again puts the window back to its modified size.

▶ Move a window using the Move command in the window's Control menu. If you have a mouse, just drag the title bar to another location.

▶ When you open a second or subsequent worksheet window, it will appear on top of the others. This makes it the active worksheet.

▶ To activate any window, select its name from the Window menu.

▶ You can switch between windows using Ctrl-F6.

▶ To view two different parts of the same worksheet, split the worksheet into two windows using the Window-New Window command.

▶ When you save a worksheet, Excel stores the window arrangements.

69

Chapter 5

Changing Your Worksheet Data

In This Chapter

71

▶ *Selecting data*
▶ *Deleting, moving, editing and copying data*
▶ *Using absolute cell references*
▶ *Inserting and deleting cells*
▶ *Using cell notes*

This chapter describes various ways you can change your worksheet data. You can edit the information in a cell, move data to other locations on the worksheet, copy information and more. These procedures will save you much time and effort when you build worksheets. You'll have the freedom to alter what you have done.

Selecting Data

A great number of Excel's commands require that you select data on the worksheet before entering the command. The command you select then applies to only the selected data. For example, to move data from one location to another requires that you first select the data to be moved, then enter the commands for moving the data. You'll find that many of the commands in this chapter and the next require data selection. So, the first thing to discuss is how to select data on the worksheet. If you have a mouse, keep an eye out for the special mouse instructions . . . you'll find them much easier than the keyboard steps.

Selecting a Cell

You've already seen how to select a single cell. Just move the cell pointer to it using any of the pointer movement commands discussed in Chapter 3. By definition, the active cell (the one on which the cell pointer is located) is selected. This means that you can't help but have at least one cell selected at all times. In fact, unless you select a range of cells, commands will often apply to the active cell because it's already selected.

72

 To select a cell with the mouse, just click in the desired cell.

Selecting a Range of Cells

Often, you'll want to select more than one cell at a time so you can apply commands to *blocks* of the worksheet. For example, you might want to change the font of a group of cells at one time. Figure 5-1 shows a selected range of cells. The following Quick Steps explain how to select a range of cells.

Q **Selecting a Range of Cells**

1. Move the pointer to the first cell of the desired range, which is the upper-left corner of the range. In Figure 5-1, you would move to cell B3.

2. Hold the Shift key down and press the arrow keys. Use the appropriate arrow keys to extend the selected area.

The highlighted range of cells grows in the direction of the arrow.

3. When the desired range is selected, release all keys.

The range is now selected. □

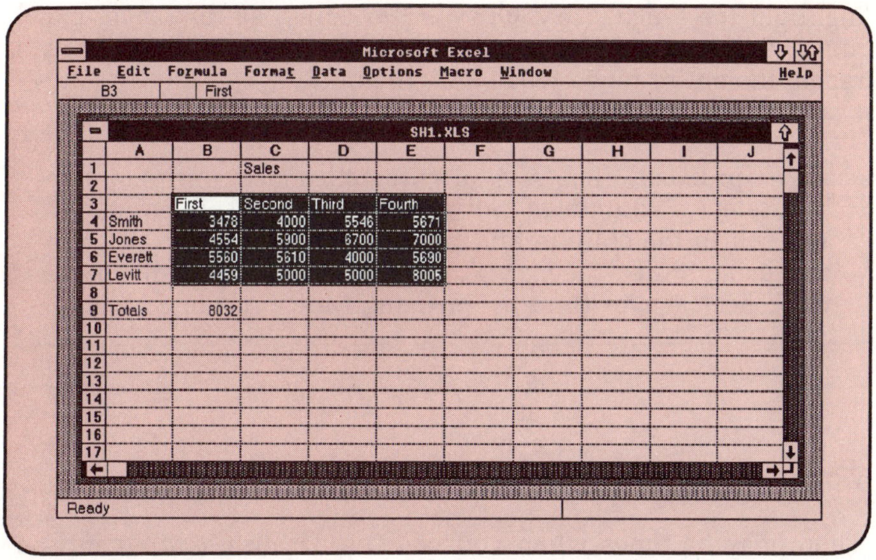

Figure 5-1. A selected range of cells appears as a highlighted block.

To select a range with the mouse, click on the first cell and hold the button, then drag the mouse to the last cell and release the button. The range between the two cells will be highlighted. Another method is to click the mouse in the first cell and release the button. Then hold the Shift key down while you click in the last cell.

The range will remain selected until you move the cell pointer again (without holding the Shift key). Try this to unselect the range.

Remember that a range of cells in a worksheet can be referenced by its first and last cells, separated by a colon. For example, the range of cells in Figure 5-1 is called B3:F9 because the upper-left cell is B3 and the lower-right cell is F9.

Another way to select a cell or range of cells is by using the Formula-Goto command. This command highlights any cell or range you specify. You might find it convenient for jumping to cells or ranges that are out of view. First, select the Goto com-

73

mand from the Formula menu. Enter the cell address or the range reference in the space marked Reference. For example, to move the cell pointer to cell Z25, type Z25 as the reference. To highlight the range Z25:Z30, type Z25:Z30 as the reference. Excel jumps to the cell or range reference you specify. If you specify a range, the entire range will be highlighted.

> ▶ **Tip:** Excel offers several automatic selections. You can select a column of cells by moving the cell pointer to any cell in the column and pressing Ctrl-Spacebar. Select a row using Shift-Spacebar. You can also select all cells in the worksheet at one time by pressing Shift-Control-Spacebar.

74 *Selecting Several Ranges*

There may be times when you want to perform a command on cells that are not adjacent. Perhaps you would like to change the font of a row along the top of the worksheet and a column along the side. To make the change to both ranges, you need to select both ranges at the same time as shown in Figure 5-2.

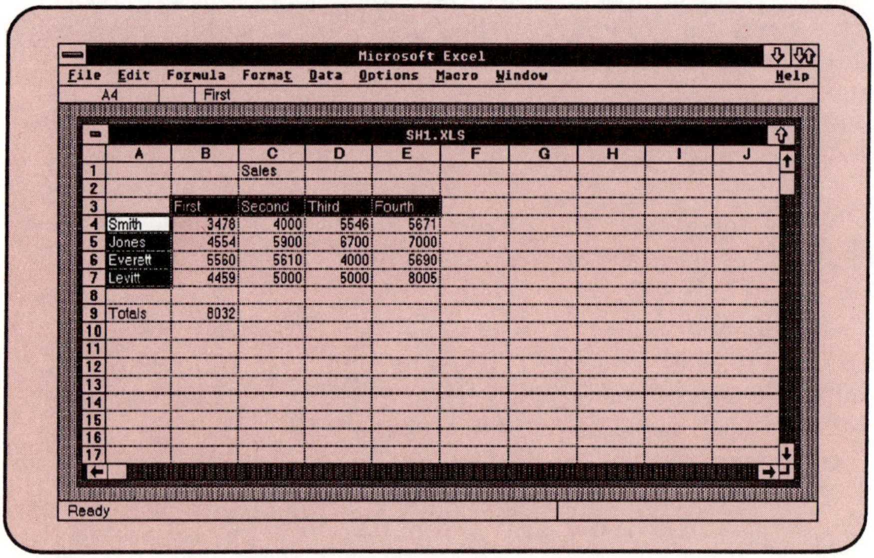

Figure 5-2. Selecting multiple ranges.

Selecting multiple ranges is an extension of the procedure for selecting a single range. The Quick Steps are described below.

Q Selecting Multiple Ranges

1. Select a range using the steps listed in the previous section.

   The selected range is highlighted.

2. Press Shift-F8.

   The status line shows the word ADD, indicating that you are adding to the currently selected range.

3. Move the pointer to the beginning of the other range. Don't use the Shift key at this time.

   The currently selected range remains selected and the pointer moves.

75

4. Press Shift with the arrow keys to highlight the next range in the usual way.

   The new range is highlighted and the first range remains highlighted.   □

To select multiple ranges with the mouse, first select a single range as described in the previous section, then press Shift-F8. Finally, select the second range as you did the first. Because you pressed Shift-F8, the first range remains selected as you select another.

You can use this procedure to highlight as many ranges as you like. As shown in Figure 5-2, the ranges can be different sizes and shapes and can be in different parts of the worksheet.

Deleting Data

Removing data from the worksheet is a common need, especially when you build large worksheets. In Excel, deleting data is known as *blanking* cells because removing data returns cells to their blank state. Like many other tasks, deleting data requires that you first select the cells that you want to blank. Following are the Quick Steps.

Deleting the Contents of a Cell or Range

1. Select the cell or range that you want to delete.

2. Select the Edit-Clear command or press the Delete key.

   The dialog box shown in Figure 5-3 appears.

3. Press A to select the All option, then press Enter.

   The All option clears all data from the selected cell or range, including entries, formatting options and notes attached to the cells.

76

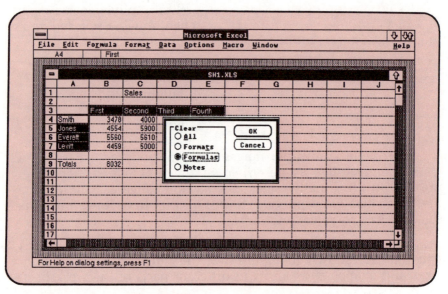

Figure 5-3. The Edit-Clear dialog box.

▶ **Tip:** If you change your mind about deleting information, you can use the Edit-Undo command to retrieve your data. Make sure you use this command immediately after deleting the information, or you might risk losing the data. Edit-Undo revokes only the most recent command performed.

Remember that you can clear the entire worksheet by first selecting all cells with the command Shift-Ctrl-Space, then using the Edit-Clear command.

Naming Cells and Ranges

You've seen how formulas often require references to cells and ranges. In fact, cell and range references are the keys to worksheet calculations. However, it can be inconvenient to use references. Often, you have to look over the worksheet to find the cell or range that you want to reference or even "scroll" through the worksheet to find data that's not in view.

By *naming* cells and ranges that you use in formulas, you can easily refer to each reference by its name. The name is easier to remember than the reference. For example, suppose you use the SUM function to add a column of values, and the formula reads =SUM(A1:A10). If you were to give the range A1:A10 the name *JANUARY*, you could add that column with the function =SUM(JANUARY). It's easier to use the name than the range reference.

77

Another advantage to range names is that they don't change when you insert or delete worksheet rows or columns. This benefit will become more clear when you read about inserting rows and columns later in this chapter.

Once you name a cell or range, you can use the name over and over throughout your worksheet formulas. To name a range, follow these Quick Steps.

Q **Naming a Range with Formula-Define Name**

1. Select the cell or range that you want to name.

   Use the commands listed earlier in this chapter to select the range.

2. Select the Formula-Define Name command.

   The dialog box shown in Figure 5-4 appears.

3. Enter the desired range name in the space labeled *Name*, then press Enter.

If a name already exists in the Name box, it will be removed when you begin typing. The existing name is Excel's guess at what the name should be. It comes from the label (if one exists) in the first cell of the range. If you like this name, simply press Enter to accept it.

78

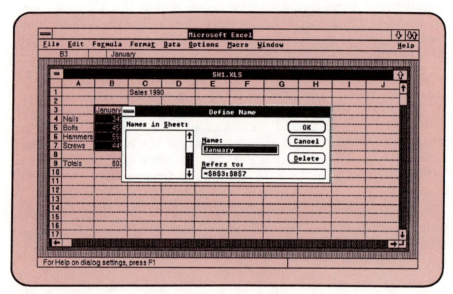

Figure 5-4. The Define Name dialog box.

Notice that the Define Name dialog box shows you a listing of all defined range names in the worksheet. The list includes the name you define, plus a few extras that appear as the result of certain operations you perform.

To use a range name in a formula, simply enter the name exactly as you typed it when you defined it. Do not use quotation marks for the reference. If you type the name incorrectly or if the name does not exist on the worksheet, Excel displays the message #NAME? in the cell to indicate it does not know the name you intend for the reference.

If you cannot remember a range name, simply use the Formula-Define Name command to display the listing of existing names. After you find the name you're looking for, press Esc to exit the dialog box.

> ▶ **Tip:** Now that you have named a cell or range, try using the Formula-Goto command to quickly jump to the named reference. Select Formula-Goto, then highlight the desired name from the list provided. When you press Enter, Excel immediately highlights the range on the worksheet. This is an excellent way of moving to specific locations on the worksheet.

Finally, here are a few pointers to remember about range names:

79

- ▶ Never use the same name twice on the same worksheet. If you do, only the second reference you named will be active.
- ▶ Upper- and lowercase letters do not matter when using range names in formulas.
- ▶ Range names must begin with a letter and can contain letters, numbers, the period, and the underscore character. Range names that look like cell references will be rejected. For example, don't name a range *A5*.
- ▶ Any part of one named range can be part of another, different named range.

Moving Data

Sometimes you may not want to completely erase data from the worksheet but instead move it to another location. You can move data using a simple two-step process. First, you cut the information from its original location, then paste it into the new location, as described in the following Quick Steps.

Q Using Cut and Paste to Move Data

1. Select the cell or range that you would like to move.

   Highlights the cell or range.

2. With the range highlighted, select the Edit-Cut command or press Shift-Delete.

   Excel places the marquee around the area to be moved. Figure 5-5 shows an example.

3. Move the pointer to the first cell of the new range into which you want to place the data. Do not select the range, just move to the upper-left corner of it. Be careful. If other data appears in this new area, it will be replaced by the moved data.

   The original range remains selected.

80

4. Press Enter or use the Edit-Paste command.

   The highlighted data moves into the new location. Figure 5-6 shows an example.

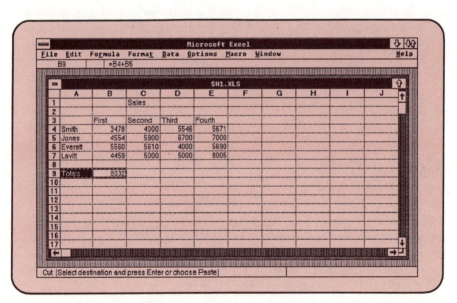

Figure 5-5.   Cutting information with the Edit-Cut command.

		Microsoft Excel								⇩ ⇧⇩
File **Edit** **Formula** **Format** **Data** **Options** **Macro** **Window**										**Help**

H9 · =B4+B5

	A	B	C	D	E	F	G	H	I	J
1			Sales							
2										
3		First	Second	Third	Fourth					
4	Smith	3478	4000	5546	5671					
5	Jones	4554	5900	6700	7000					
6	Everett	5560	5610	4000	5690					
7	Levitt	4459	5000	5000	8005					
8										
9							Totals	8032		
10										
11										
12										
13										
14										
15										
16										
17										

Ready

81

Figure 5-6.   The result of moving data.

When you move cells that contain cell references, the references remain exactly as they were in the original location. Take another look at Figure 5-5 and notice that the formula in cell B9 is showing in the formula bar. The formula contains a reference to another cell. When the data in cell B9 is moved as shown in Figure 5-6, the formula and its reference remain the same. The fact that references do not change might not surprise you, since it is probably what you would expect to happen. However, there are times when you want cell references to adjust to new locations. The section *Copying Data* later in this chapter describes how to move data so that cell references adjust.

> ► **Tip:** If you cut and move a cell that has a reference to another cell, the reference will remain the same when pasted to a new location. The cell continues to reference the same data. However, if you cut and paste a cell that is being referenced by another cell, the reference changes to reflect the new location of the referenced cell. For example, suppose cell A4 contains a reference to cell A1. If you cut cell A1 and paste it to cell H5, cell A4 will now reference H5. Excel makes this adjustment so that the cell containing a reference continues to reference the same data, even after the data has been moved.

Editing Data

Once you have entered information into a cell and accepted it, how do you change the data? Well, there are two ways. One way is to completely retype the entry. Simply move the pointer to the cell, type your new entry and press Enter to accept it. When you accept the new entry, it replaces the old one.

The second way to change the data is to edit the data currently in the cell. You can change the existing entry, then save the changes you make. These changes are carried out in the formula bar using a series of editing commands.

First, move the pointer to the cell that you want to change. The contents of the cell appear in the formula bar. Press F2 to shift control to the formula bar, where a flashing cursor appears. Figure 5-7 shows an example. Next, use the editing commands to change the data in the formula bar. Editing commands are listed in Table 5-1. Press Enter to accept the changes or Esc to reject them. If you accept the changes, Excel updates the information in the cell.

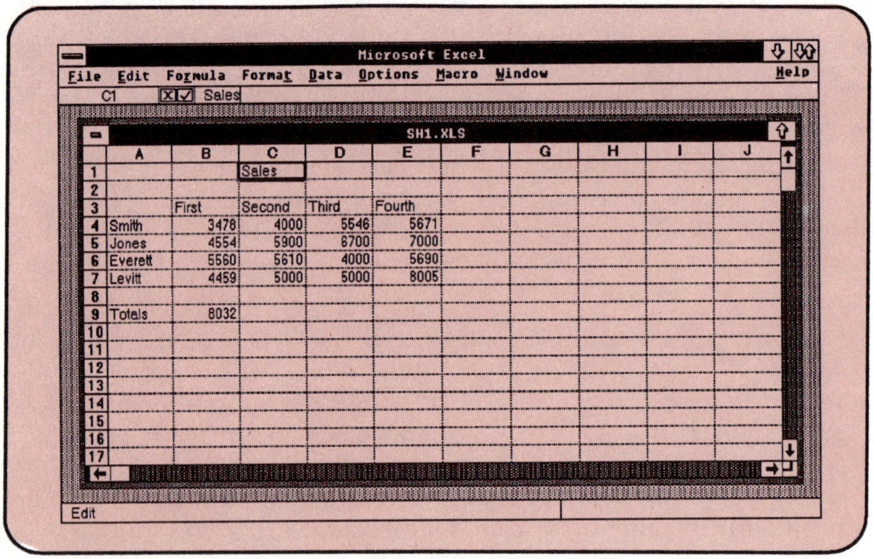

82

Figure 5-7. Pressing F2 places the cursor in the formula bar.

Table 5-1. **Editing Commands**

Key	Result
← or →	Moves one character left or right
↑ or ↓	Moves one line up or down (if there is more than one line)
Delete	Removes the character to the right of the cursor
Backspace	Removes the character to the left of the cursor
[type]	Type to insert new text at the cursor position
Home	Moves to the beginning of the entry
End	Moves to the end of the entry
Enter	Accepts the changes
Esc	Rejects the changes

Copying Data

To avoid retyping information on the worksheet, you can copy it over and over again. Copying data is similar to moving data. When data is copied, the original entry remains intact and a duplicate is placed in a new location. Excel offers several ways to copy information. This section will show you three different methods of copying data. Plus, it will discuss some important facts about copying formulas.

The Edit-Copy Command

Using the example in Figure 5-8, suppose you want to copy the headings First, Second, Third and Fourth from the 1990 section over to the 1991 section. This would save you the time of retyping those headings for the 1991 totals. You can use the Edit-Copy command to copy the headings, as described in the following Quick Steps.

 Copying with the Edit-Copy Command

1. Select the range of cells   In Figure 5-8, you would
   that you want to copy.   select the range B3:E3.

2. Select the Edit-Copy command.

The copy marquee will surround the highlighted range, as shown in Figure 5-9. Notice the message in the status bar at the bottom of the screen.

3. Move the pointer to the first cell in the range that will receive the copy. This should be the upper-left corner of the range.

The marquee will remain on the original information.

4. Press Enter to copy the data to the new location.

The original data will remain in place and a copy will appear at the pointer location. Figure 5-10 shows the result. ☐

84

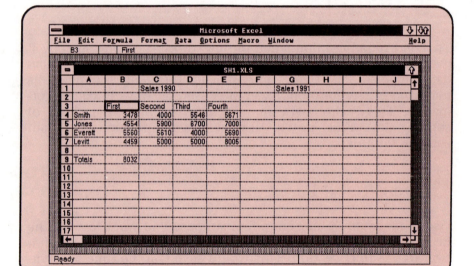

Figure 5-8.   A sample worksheet ready for copying.

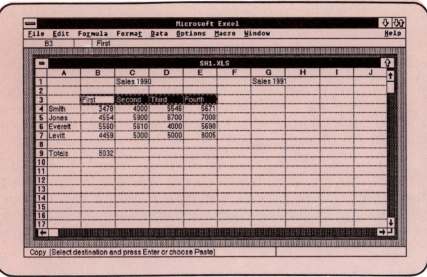

Figure 5-9. Copying the highlighted range using Edit-Copy.

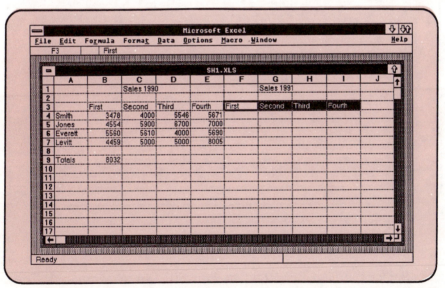

Figure 5-10. The worksheet after copying data to the new location.

Edit-Fill Right and Edit-Fill Down

You can copy numbers, text or formulas using the Edit-Copy command. But you might find it convenient to copy formulas with the Edit-Fill Right and Edit-Fill Down commands. While these commands will copy any type of data, they are especially useful for copying a formula across a row (Fill Right) or down a column (Fill Down). (Excel also offers the similar Edit-Fill Left and Edit-Fill Up commands.)

To use Edit-Fill Right or Edit-Fill Down, start by moving the pointer to the cell with the formula that you want to copy. Using the mouse or key commands, highlight the range into which you want to copy the formula. This range must include the original cell, plus cells to the right or down that will contain the copies. Figure 5-11 shows an example.

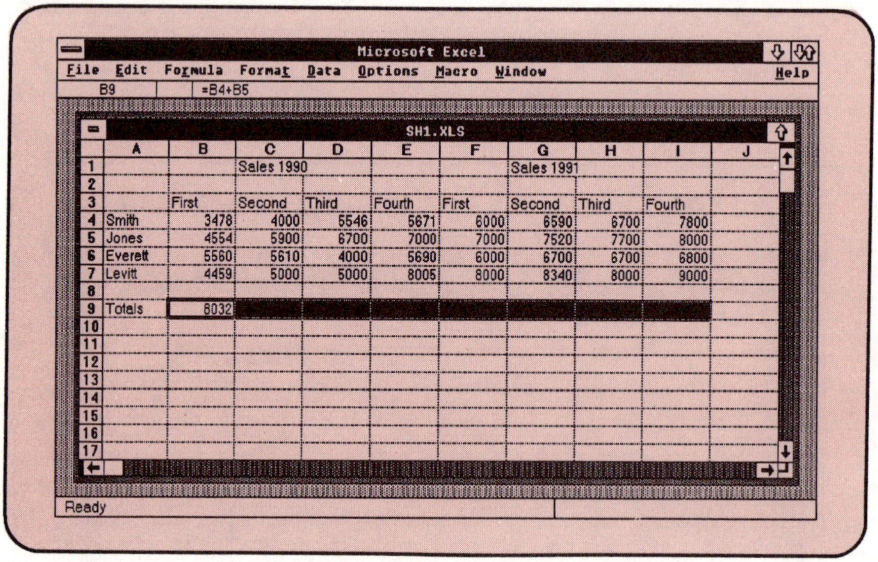

86

Figure 5-11. Highlighting the range to copy, including the original cell.

Select the Edit-Fill Right or Edit-Fill Down command. The formula in the first cell is instantly copied to the remaining cells in the highlighted range. Figure 5-12 shows the result.

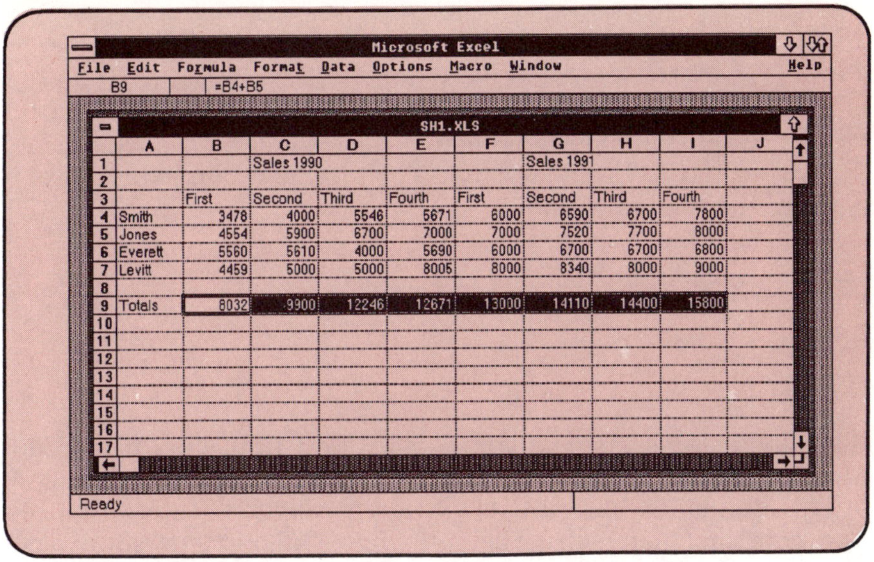

Figure 5-12. The result of the Edit-Fill Right command.

87

As you can see, these commands are especially useful for copying formulas, but you can use them to copy any data from one cell to many adjacent cells. When copying a formula, keep in mind that cell references will adjust for each copy's new location. For example, the new formulas in Figure 5-12 produce the totals of their respective columns, not the total of the first column. If you examine the formulas that were copied, you'll notice that each has been adjusted to total the column where it's located. The formula in cell C9 is `=SUM(C4:C7)`. The formula in D9 is `=SUM(D4:D7)`.

A condition called *relative referencing* allows Excel to automatically adjust formula references (such as matching the columns in the preceding example). Relative referencing is useful for situations like the one shown in Figure 5-12. However, you might find the need to prevent this automatic adjustment when you use the Edit-Copy or Edit-Fill Right command. Preventing relative referencing is discussed in the section *Absolute Referencing* later in this chapter.

> ▶ **Tip:** As you learned earlier, the Cut command does not use relative referencing like the Copy command. If you want to move data using the Cut and Paste procedure, but you want relative referencing, use the Copy command instead of the Cut command. Then, remove the extra copy from the original location.

The Ctrl-Enter Technique

Let's look at one more way to copy information. You might find this technique the most convenient for many situations. You can copy information as you enter it by pressing Ctrl-Enter to repeat the data in other cells. The following Quick Steps show you how.

88

Q **Copying with Ctrl-Enter**

1. Select the range of cells where you want to place the data. The entire range should be empty.

   The range is highlighted and the first cell is active.

2. Enter the number, text or formula into the active cell.

   The data you enter appears in the formula bar.

3. Press Ctrl-Enter to accept the formula.

   Copies the entry to all cells in the highlighted range. ☐

The result of using Ctrl-Enter is similar to the results from the Edit-Fill commands, but you can perform this copy technique as you enter the first formula, rather than afterward.

Using Absolute Cell References

You've seen how cell and range references adjust when you copy formulas. This is called relative referencing, and it is a useful feature that saves you from typing formulas over and over.

Most cell and range references are relative unless you make them *absolute*. (When you define a name for a range or reference, the default is absolute referencing.) An absolute reference does not change when the formula is copied to another cell. To make a reference absolute, simply insert dollar signs between the row and column references, as in the following examples:

$A$1	Absolute column and row
$A1	Absolute column but relative row
A$1	Relative column but absolute row
$A$1:$C$3	Absolute range reference

Notice that references can be partially relative and partially absolute. These mixed references are useful for special types of copying needs where the row reference may change, but the column reference will remain absolute (or vice versa). You may not find an occasion to use mixed references.

89

Let's take a look at a basic absolute reference. Take the worksheet shown in Figure 5-13. This worksheet calculates the total price of three different items given each item's price per carton (entered into column C) and a desired quantity (entered into cell B3). Simply change the quantity value in cell B3 to calculate the total income from an order. The formula for the total in cell B6 is =C6*B3. This multiplies the carton price of the item by the given quantity.

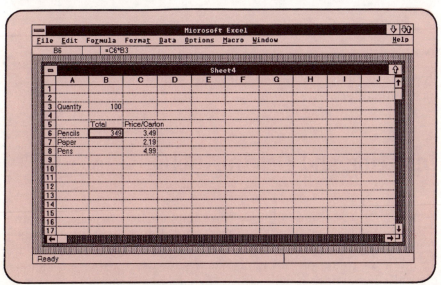

Figure 5-13. A simple worksheet example of relative referencing.

Copying the formula =C6*B3 to the remaining cells in column B would produce errors. While the new formulas in cells B7 and B8 should reference the respective carton prices from column C, both formulas should reference exactly the same quantity amount from cell B3. This requires that the reference to cell B3 be absolute. Figure 5-14 shows the correct reference contained in cell B8 after making the reference to cell B3 absolute before copying.

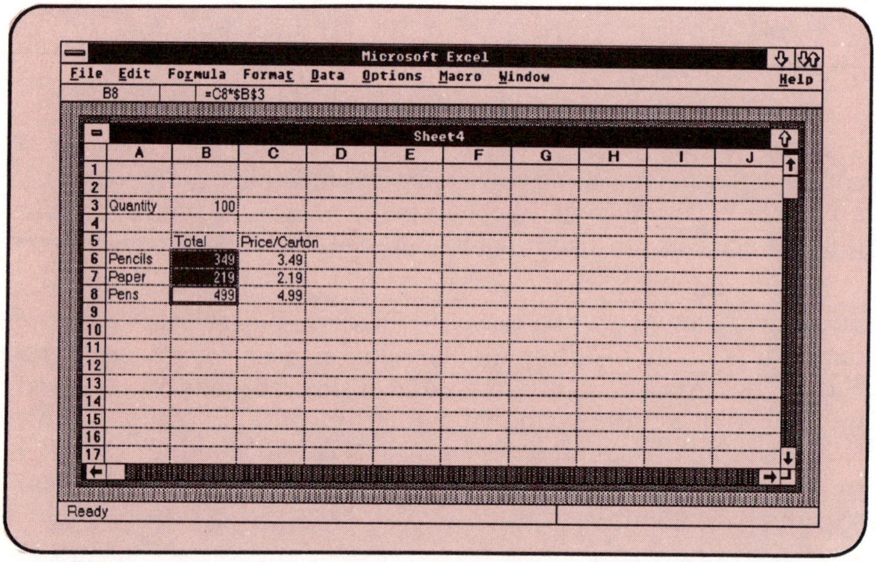

Figure 5-14. Copying with absolute references.

Remember that relative cell references only change when they are copied, not when they are moved with the Cut and Paste procedure. All references are absolute when moved.

Inserting and Deleting Cells

You can add rows and columns to your worksheet or remove them when needed using the Edit-Insert and Edit-Delete commands. Often, inserting extra columns or rows is necessary to make room for additional data or formulas. When you insert a row, for example, all rows below it will shift down to make room. When you delete rows, all rows below the deleted ones shift up to fill the space. Likewise, you might find the need to delete rows or columns from a worksheet to close up some empty space.

For example, to use Edit-Insert, start by moving the pointer to the row where you would like to insert a new row. Press Shift-Spacebar to highlight this row. If you want to insert more than one row, press Shift-↓ to highlight more. Highlight as many rows as you want Excel to insert. Figure 5-15 shows a worksheet ready for inserting.

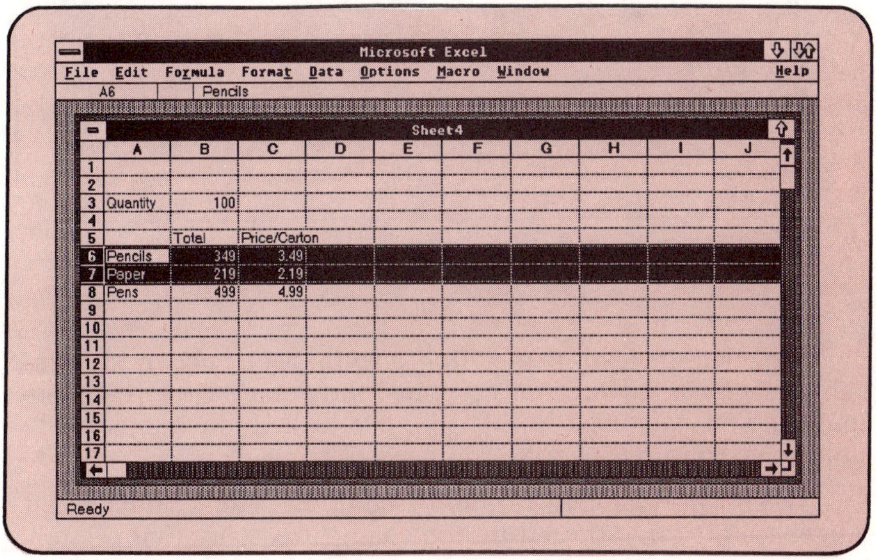

91

*Figure 5-15. **Worksheet rows highlighted for the insert command.***

If you have a mouse, you can accomplish the previous steps by clicking on the row heading number (on the left border of the worksheet), holding the mouse button down and then dragging down to highlight as many rows as you like. Release the button when finished.

Select the Edit-Insert command. Excel inserts as many rows as you have highlighted and shifts all existing rows down to make room. Figure 5-16 shows the result.

Of course, you can perform the same process for columns by highlighting columns instead of rows. Highlight a column using the command Ctrl-Spacebar.

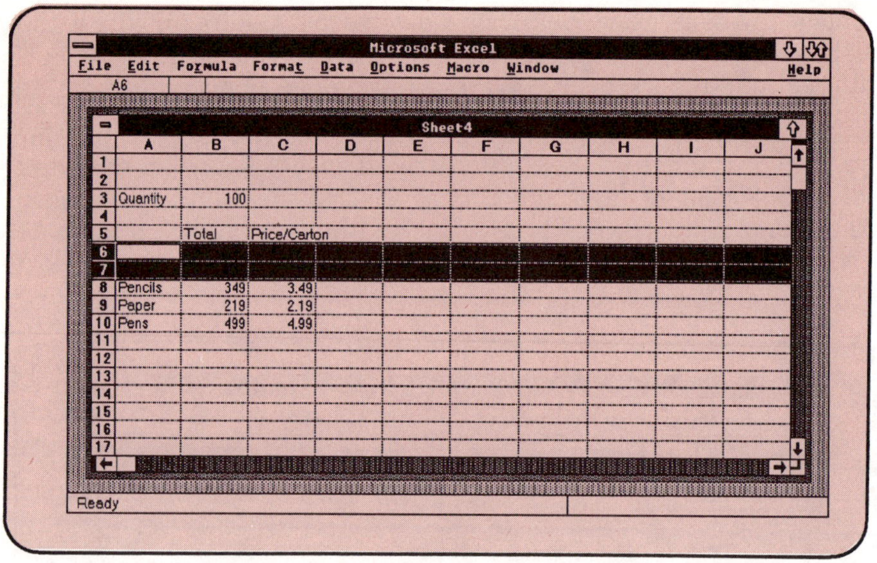

92

Figure 5-16.   The result of the Edit-Insert command.

To delete instead of inserting, use the steps above to high-light the unwanted rows or columns, then enter the Edit-Delete command. If you make a mistake, use Edit-Undo immediately after deleting to retrieve the rows or columns.

When you insert rows and/or columns, Excel adjusts cell references that are affected by the change to assure that the for-mulas continue to produce the intended values. For example, a formula might refer to cell B4 prior to inserting a row. After you insert a row above cell B4, this cell becomes B5, and the refer-ence to it automatically changes to B5.

Applying Cell Notes

Cell notes are a valuable tool when using worksheets. If you create worksheets to share with others, cell notes are almost a must for helping other operators use your worksheet properly. But cell notes also can be practical for your own, private worksheets. Cell notes can help remind you of the purpose behind formulas or of the information that you are supposed to enter in various locations. Or cell notes can provide detailed information about values used in a worksheet. The following Quick Steps explain how to add a note to a cell.

Q Adding a Note to a Cell

1. Move the pointer to the desired cell.

2. Select the Formula-Note command.

    Excel presents the dialog box shown in Figure 5-17.

3. Type the note in the space provided. To move to a new line, use Ctrl-Enter to move the cursor down. If you make mistakes while typing, use the Backspace key to correct them. Also, you may use the editing commands listed in Table 5-1.

    The text of the note will fit into the box.

4. Press Enter to accept the note.

93

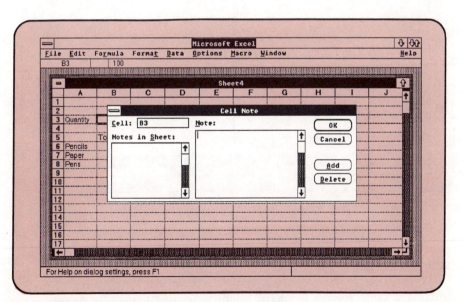

Figure 5-17. Adding a cell note.

Besides displaying the note attached to the active cell, the note dialog box lists all notes that have been added to cells in the active worksheet. These notes appear in the Notes in Sheet box. Excel shows the cell containing the note and the first line of each note to remind you of its contents.

You can edit any note by moving to the appropriate cell and selecting the Formula-Note command again. This displays the cell's note in the dialog box where you can change it. You can also select one of the notes in the Notes in Sheet listing to view the entire note, even if the pointer is not on that cell. After making changes, remember to press Enter to accept them or Esc to reject them.

You can display a cell's note using the Window-Show Info command. Start by moving the pointer to the desired cell. Select the Window-Show Info command. This brings up the Info display as shown in Figure 5-18.

94

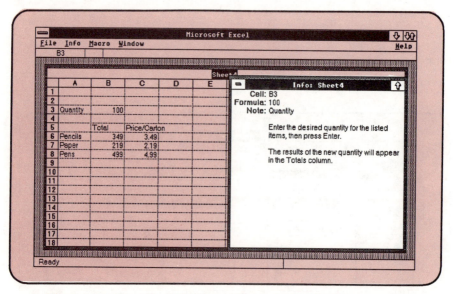

Figure 5-18. The Window-Show Info display.

This Info window shows various information about the active cell, including its note, any formula in the cell and the cell's address. Since this display is a window and not a dialog box, you can change its size, shape and position as you would any window. Chapter 4 describes how to manipulate windows.

> ▶ **Tip:** While the Info window is active, you can choose other information to display by using the commands in the Info menu.

What You've Learned

This chapter provided details about editing information in the worksheet using various editing commands. It also showed you how to copy, move, insert and delete data using various commands in the Edit menu. The use of relative and absolute cell references plays an important role in copying formulas. Following are some points to remember:

95

- ▶ Use the Shift key with the cursor movement keys to select ranges of cells. Selected ranges are highlighted and are available for various commands.
- ▶ Select a row by pressing Shift-Spacebar and a column by pressing Ctrl-Spacebar. Select all cells at once by pressing Shift-Ctrl-Spacebar.
- ▶ Ranges are referenced by their first and last cells, separated by a colon. These represent two opposite corners of the range, as in A1:D4.
- ▶ Use the Edit-Clear command to delete information in selected cells.
- ▶ To move data from one location to another, use the Cut and Paste commands. First use Edit-Cut, then press Enter to paste.
- ▶ Press F2 to edit the contents of a cell. Then use the various editing commands.
- ▶ When copying a formula, cell references contained in that formula will be copied relative to their new locations.
- ▶ You can copy data with the Edit-Copy command, the Edit-Fill Down command or the Edit-Fill Right command.
- ▶ You can prevent the relative copying of cell references by making references absolute. To make a reference absolute,

add dollar signs to its column and row references, as in $A$1.

▶ To insert or delete rows or columns of cells, use the Edit-Insert and Edit-Delete commands after selecting the appropriate rows or columns.

▶ Cell notes are useful for providing detailed information about a cell's contents. To add a note, move to the desired cell and select the Formula-Note command.

▶ Display a cell's note using the Window-Show Info command.

96

Enhancing the Appearance of Data

In This Chapter

- ▶ *Changing fonts, sizes and styles*
- ▶ *Special characters*
- ▶ *Aligning data*
- ▶ *Formatting numbers, dates and times*
- ▶ *Rounding numbers*
- ▶ *Changing the worksheet display*
- ▶ *Adding borders to cells*

This chapter deals with enhancements you can make to the appearance of data on the worksheet. You can manipulate fonts, alter the color of data on the screen and make various other formatting changes. Here you can learn about many of Excel's formatting options to make your worksheets more attractive and readable. You'll find many of these features useful for all your worksheets.

Changing Fonts, Sizes and Styles

A font is a style of printing or type. Excel comes with several different fonts ready for use, and you can switch between them at any time. Figure 6-1 shows the various fonts that come with Excel.

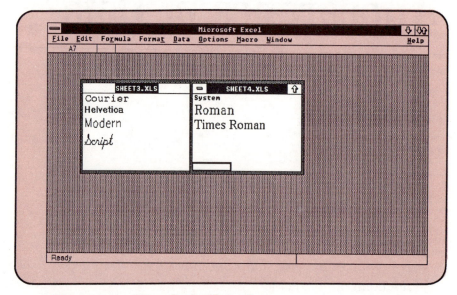

Figure 6-1. Excel's built-in fonts.

Excel's fonts can be displayed at various sizes and in various styles. Styles include boldface, italics, underline and strike-out. In Figure 6-1, the fonts are displayed with no styles active.

Excel lets you have up to four different fonts on any worksheet at one time. Alternatively, you can have the same font in four different styles active at one time. Or you can have some combination of fonts and styles—up to four different fonts and/or styles at one time.

To make opening a worksheet easy, Excel comes with four fonts and styles selected. These are called the *default fonts*. Of course, you can pick and choose the four fonts and styles you would like by accessing and changing the default fonts. The next sections show you how to access and change the default fonts to four different fonts.

Default Fonts, Sizes and Styles

The four default fonts are:

Font 1: Helvetica 10
Font 2: Helvetica 10 boldface
Font 3: Helvetica 10 italic
Font 4: Helvetica 10 bold-italic

The default fonts are shown in Figure 6-2. Note that Font 1 is the font that appears automatically when you begin typing data onto the worksheet. In other words, if you don't switch to a different font, this is the font you'll get.

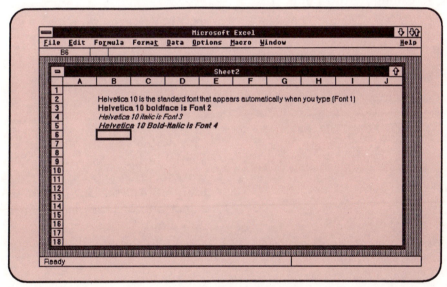

Figure 6-2.   The default fonts in action.

You can change the font of existing data, or set the font of a cell before you begin typing. Remember that each cell can be formatted with a different one of these four fonts. You can select a range of cells and then change the font if desired.

To switch among the default fonts, use the following keystrokes after selecting the desired cells:

Ctrl-1   Font 1
Ctrl-2   Font 2
Ctrl-3   Font 3
Ctrl-4   Font 4

Customizing the Fonts, Sizes and Styles

The four default fonts are useful for many worksheets. But you can select four different fonts if you like. You can change fonts using the following Quick Steps.

 Changing the Fonts

100

1. Select the Format-Font command.

   The four active fonts appear in a dialog box as shown in Figure 6-3.

2. To change Font 1, press 1. To change one of the other fonts, highlight the desired font.

   Highlights the first option in the box.

3. Press O to display the available fonts.

   The dialog box displays all available fonts for your worksheet as shown in Figure 6-4. You can now select one of these as the new Font 1.

4. Use the ↑ or ↓ key to highlight the desired font name, then press Tab twice.

   Moves to the Size list.

5. Use the ↑ or ↓ key to select a size from the list, then press Tab once.

   Moves to the Styles options.

6. Select any or all of the four styles by typing the letter associated with the style name. Combining styles is perfectly okay.

7. Press Enter when finished.

□

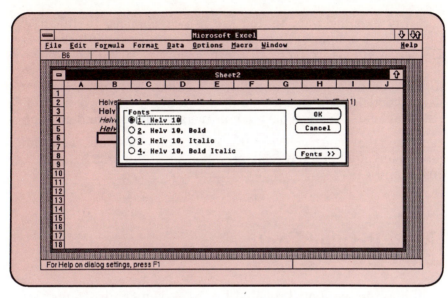

Figure 6-3.   The four active fonts are shown in the Format-Fonts dialog box.

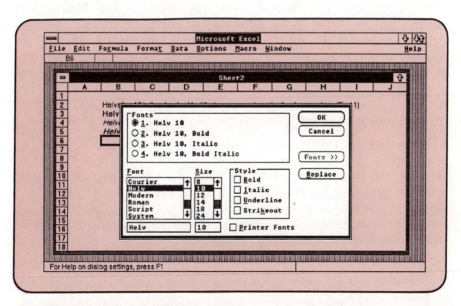

Figure 6-4.   Additional fonts appear when you select the Fonts option.

Any existing data in the worksheet changes to the new fonts. For example, all data entered in the default Font 1 (Helvetica 10) will change to the new Font 1 (whatever you've set). For this reason, it's a good idea to leave Font 1 as Helvetica 10 or some other small font. Since boldface is so common, it's also a good idea to make Font 2 a boldface version of Font 1. This way, you'll always have a bold version of the standard font.

Now that you have set the new group of fonts, you can choose any font for any cell or range by typing Ctrl-1, Ctrl-2, Ctrl-3, and Ctrl-4.

Using Printer Fonts

102

In addition to the fonts provided by Excel, you can use fonts that are designed especially for your printer. If you have a laser printer, you may have several fonts or font cartridges that work with it. With Excel, it's best to use the printer fonts for quick and problem-free printing. To use the printer fonts, first use the File-Printer Setup command to make sure the correct printer is selected. (If the desired printer is not on the Printer Setup list, refer to Chapter 8 for details about adding printers to the list.) Use the Setup option in the File-Printer Setup command to establish the various options and fonts that you want to use with the printer. When you return to the worksheet after setting up the printer, you can use the printer fonts on the worksheet data.

To use the printer fonts, select the Format-Font command and choose the Fonts option by pressing O. Finally, check the box marked Printer Fonts by pressing Alt-P. After you check this box, the printer fonts should appear in the font listing in the dialog box. You can now use these fonts as you would any built-in fonts provided by Excel. To return to using the Excel fonts, simply uncheck the Printer Fonts box.

> ▶ **Note:** If Excel does not have a screen version of the printer font you select, it will substitute a font from the same class. In such a case, the printout may look different than the screen.

Using Special Characters

Excel gives you access to many special characters that do not appear on the keyboard and are sometimes known as the extended character set. The extended character set includes many international characters, accented characters, and special symbols. You might have an occasion to use these characters in your worksheets. Figure 6-5 shows the extended character set.

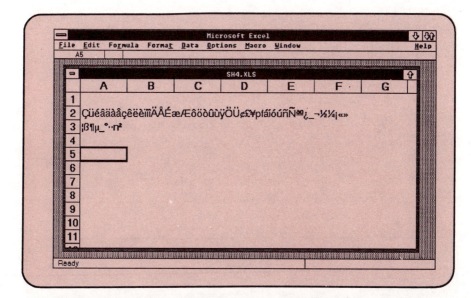

Figure 6-5. Excel's special characters.

103

For a list of extended characters, see an ASCII chart in your DOS or system manual. The extended characters are numbered from 129 to 255.

Special characters are entered by pressing the Alt key along with an ASCII code number. For example, typing Alt-155 produces the character ¢ (cents symbol). Just hold down the Alt key and enter the number 155 on the numeric keypad, then release all keys. The character will appear in the formula bar.

The ability to print these characters depends on your printer. Experiment for best results. You might find that you can see special characters on the screen but can't print them.

Aligning Information in a Cell

When entered into a cell, numbers and dates automatically align with the right side of the cell. Similarly, text aligns itself with the left side of the cell. While these alignments suit most needs, you can change the alignment of information at any time. Simply select the information, then use the Format-Alignment command as described in the following Quick Steps.

Q Aligning Cells with Format-Alignment

1. Select the cell or cells that contain the data you want to align.

104

2. Select the Format-Alignment command.

   The alignment dialog box shown in Figure 6-6 appears.

3. Choose the desired alignment from the list and press Enter to make the change.

   The selected data conforms to the alignment you choose.

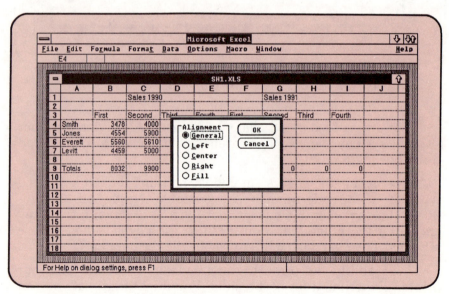

Figure 6-6.   Alignment options.

Following are explanations of the various alignment options:

General	Aligns numbers and dates with the right side of the cell and text with the left side.
Left	Aligns selected data with the left side of the cell
Center	Centers data within the cell
Right	Aligns data with the right side of the cell
Fill	Repeats the data to fill the entire width of the cell

Remember that the current cell widths affect alignment. The wider the cell, the more dramatic any alignment selections will appear.

You can remove the alignment you've added to a cell or range by changing it back to the General alignment setting. Alternatively, you can use the Edit-Clear command and choose the Formats option from the Clear dialog box. This clears only the alignment, fonts and other formatting attached to the cell.

105

When you copy or move aligned data, the alignment is copied or moved along with the rest of the data. You can prevent copying alignment by using the Edit-Paste Special option with the Formulas or Values option to paste the data into the new location.

Number Formats

In Chapter 3 you saw how number entries can begin with or include special characters, such as $ % − and (. Some of these symbols actually change the format of the value you enter, although they don't change the value itself. Table 6-1 shows some examples.

As you can see from the table, entering a dollar sign along with a value formats the value by including the dollar symbol, rounding to two decimal places and displaying negative numbers in parentheses. This is a traditional dollar-value format. When you add a percent sign to the end of the value, Excel dis-

Table 6-1. Symbols Affecting Number Formats

You type	Excel displays	Actual value in cell
5.999	5.999	5.999
$5.999	$6.00	5.999
−$5.999	($6.00)	−5.999
(5.999)	−5.999	−5.999
5%	5%	0.05

plays the value as a percentage and converts the percentage value to a decimal equivalent. The decimal equivalent of 5% is .05.

But dollar values and percentages are not the only formats you can use for numbers. They are simply the ones you can control *as you type the value*. You can set the format of any existing values on the worksheet using Excel's Format-Number command as the following Quick Steps describe.

106

Q Formatting Values with Format-Number

1. Select the cell or range that contains the data you want to format.

2. Select the Format-Number command.

   Excel presents a list of formats available for your data, as shown in Figure 6-7.

3. Choose a format from the list and press Enter.

   The selected data conforms to the chosen format. ☐

The items in Figure 6-7 look pretty obscure don't they? Without some background it's difficult to tell what each of these formats does. Well, the list contains three groups of formats: for numbers, for dates and for times. Let's look at the number formats in this list (the other formats will be covered later). Table 6-2 shows the various formats listed in the Format-Number dialog box and their effect on worksheet values.

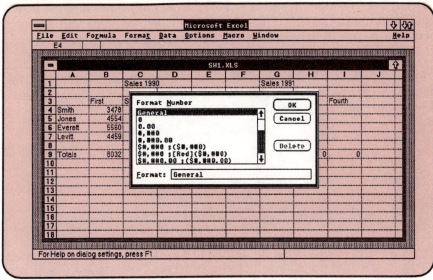

Figure 6-7.   Excel's number formats.

107

Table 6-2.   Excel's Number Formats

Format	Positive Display	Negative Display	Zero Display
General	3595.5	−3595.5	0
0	3596	−3596	0
0.00	3595.50	−3595.50	0.00
#,###0	3,596	−3,596	0
#.###0.00	3,595.50	−3,595.50	0.00
$#,##0;($#,##0)	$3,596	($3,596)	$0
$#,##0;[RED]($#,##0)	$3,596	($3,596)*	$0
$#,##0.00;($#,##0.00)	$3,595.50	($3,595.50)	$0.00
$#,##0.00;[RED]($#,##0.00)	$3,595.50	($3,595.50)*	$0.00
0%	359550%	−359550%	0%
0.00%	359550.00%	−359550.00%	0.00%
0.00E+00	3.60E+03	−3.60E+03	0.00E+00

*Displays in red, if available

second for negative numbers. Later this chapter explains how you can customize these formats to control how zero values and text values are displayed when entered into a cell.

Excel provides a shortcut method for selecting the most common formats. First, highlight the cell or range containing the data to be formatted, then press one of the following key combinations to get the format listed beside it:

Ctrl-~	General
Ctrl-!	0.00
Ctrl-$	$#,##0;($#,##0)
Ctrl-%	0%
Ctrl-^	0.00E+00

108

You'll probably find the shortcuts for changing formats easiest, and the five formats selected with the shortcuts are the most commonly used of all. Hence, you can avoid using the Format-Numbers listing almost entirely.

In addition to formatting data already in the worksheet, you can preformat a block of blank cells using one of the number formats. Whenever you enter a value into one of the preformatted cells, it will automatically apply to the format you selected.

To erase a format that has been applied to a cell or range, select the cell or range and enter the Edit-Clear command. When the dialog box appears, select the Formats option and press Enter. This procedure removes any formatting attached to the cells, including font formatting. To remove only number formatting, select all the cells and choose the General format.

When you copy or move cells that have been formatted, the formatting stays with the data. If you want to copy the data without the formatting, use the Edit-Paste Special command to paste the data into the new location (instead of Edit-Paste or Enter). Then, select the Formulas or Values option and press Enter.

Date and Time Formats

Chapter 3 described how you can enter dates in a few different ways so that Excel will accept the date and display it in a particular format. Dates can be entered as shown in Table 6-3.

Table 6-3. Entering Dates

You type	Excel displays
12/1/91	12/1/91
12-1-91	12/1/91
1 Dec 91	1-Dec-91
1-Dec-91	1-Dec-91
1 December 1991	1-Dec-91
December 91	Dec-91
1 December	1-Dec
1 Dec	1-Dec
12/1	1-Dec
12-1	1-Dec

109

Although you should enter all dates using one of the formats in Table 6-3, you can change the way Excel displays the date if you like. First, enter the date using one of the formats shown in Table 6-3. Next, select the cell containing the date and then choose one of the date formats from the Format-Numbers listing. The date formats appear below the list of number formats. Date formats and an example of each are listed in Table 6-4.

Table 6-4. Date Formats

Format Listing	Example
m/d/yy	1/23/89
d-mmm-yy	23-Jan-89
d-mmm	23-Jan
mmm-yy	Jan-89

As you can see, each of the date formats in Table 6-4 can be achieved when you enter the date in the first place. Just choose the associated entry format. However, it's nice to know that you can change any date at any time.

Like dates, times can be entered into Excel using one of several entry methods. Table 6-5 shows the time formats you can use.

Table 6-5. Entering Times

You type	Excel displays
15:35	15:35
4:35	4:35
4:35:15	4:35:15
4:35 pm	4:35 PM
4:35:15 am	4:35:15 AM

110

Excel assumes the 24-hour time format unless you enter the am or pm designation. Like date formats, time formats are most easily achieved by entering the time in the correct way. However, you can change the format of a time by highlighting the desired cell and using the Format-Time listing. The time formats are listed in Table 6-6.

Table 6-6. Time Formats

Format Listing	Example
h:mm AM/PM	9:35 PM
h:mm:ss AM/PM	9:35:15 PM
h:mm	21:35
h:mm:ss	21:35:15

Hiding Values of Zero

Worksheets often have zeros all over the place as the result of calculations or unentered information. Formulas often display a zero when referenced cells are blank. These zeros can make a worksheet look confusing and cluttered. Figure 6-8 shows a worksheet with several columns where data has not been entered. Therefore, the cells with the formulas that total the empty columns produce zeros. In such a case, you might want to suppress the zeros.

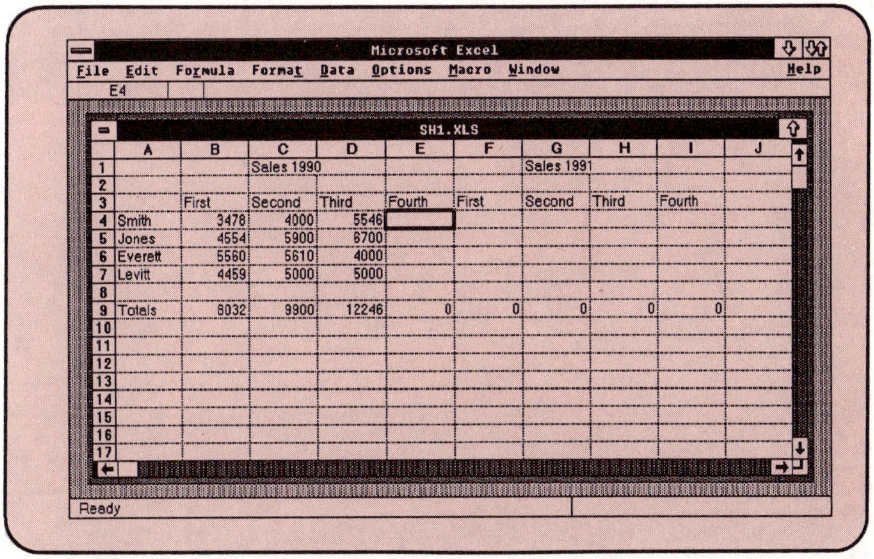

Figure 6-8.   Example of formulas that produce unwanted values of zero.

You can make all values of zero appear as blank cells by using the Options-Display command. After selecting this command, the dialog box in Figure 6-9 appears. You have several choices at this point. This time, select the Zero Values option. (Other options in the Options-Display dialog box are discussed later in this chapter.) Press Z to remove the check mark from the option, causing the zero values to display as blanks on the worksheet.

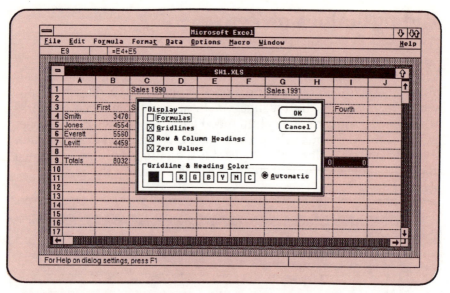

Figure 6-9. *The Options-Display dialog box.*

112

The result is that all zeros contained in this worksheet are invisible. Making all zero values invisible can clean up the appearance of the worksheet for printouts and display purposes. However, you might find the need to suppress only some of the zero values in a worksheet, leaving others alone. In this case, you can use a special formatting technique to affect only selected cells. The following Quick Steps explain this process.

Q Suppressing Zeros in Specific Cells

1. Select the cell or range that you want to change.

2. Select the Format-Numbers command.

   The Format-Numbers dialog box appears.

3. Press the Tab key to highlight the Format entry box at the bottom of the dialog box.

   Excel highlights the format currently applied to the selected cells. Unless you've changed it, this will be the General format. The screen should look like Figure 6-10.

4. Press the → key to move the cursor to the end of the entry. Now type `;-GENERAL;`, assuming the entry shows the General format. If some other format is showing in the dialog box, see the explanation that follows for the modification you need to make.

The result should look like Figure 6-11.

□

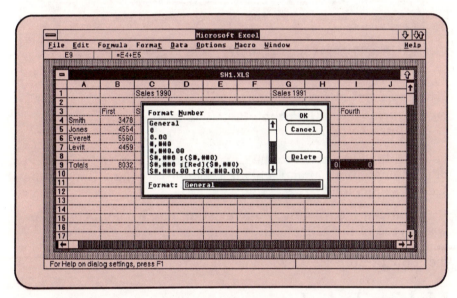

113

Figure 6-10. Ready to change the current format in the Format-Numbers dialog box.

In the preceding Quick Steps, you actually modified the General number format so that it displays zeros differently than other values (in this case, it doesn't display them at all). Number formats are divided into parts that are separated by semicolons. If a format has only one part (no semicolons), it applies to all values. If a format has two parts (one semicolon), the first part applies to positive values and zeros, and the second part applies to negative values. If the format has three parts (two semicolons), the first part applies to positive values, the second part to negative values, and the third part to zero values. In these steps,

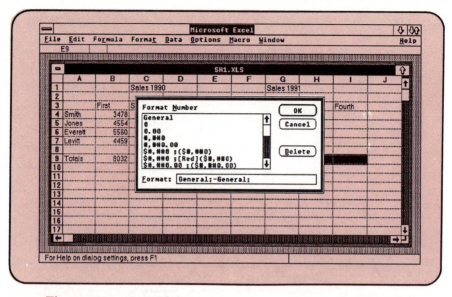

114

Figure 6-11.   Modifying the General format so it suppresses zeros.

you've added two parts to the General format: a negative version of the General format and a blank version (nothing following the second semicolon).

You can modify any of the existing number formats in this way. Some of the formats already have two parts, in which case you need only add the third. Remember that semicolons divide the format into parts.

Making Data Invisible and Other Custom Formats

Modifying number formats can be useful for making them suppress zeros. However, you might be interested in creating some completely original number formats for special purposes. One example is to create a format that makes all values invisible to hide information on a worksheet.

Perhaps a worksheet contains entries that are confidential but needed for making calculations. You can hide the values from view without removing them from the worksheet using the ;;; number format. Just select the desired data, choose the Format-

Numbers command, press the Tab key to highlight the entry area and type the format as *;;;* (three semicolons). The entire format should consist of only three semicolons. Press Enter to accept the custom format, and the highlighted data becomes invisible. To make the data reappear, simply change the data's format to any other in the list.

▶ **Tip:** All modified and custom number formats can be re-used within a worksheet without retyping them. Excel remembers all special formats and stores them along with the others in the Format-Numbers listing. Your customized formats appear at the bottom of the list, so you can select them again and again. If you create a custom format for one worksheet, you have to recreate the format on other worksheets.

Another useful format controls the way phone numbers appear on the worksheet. To try this out, enter a 10-digit number in any cell of the worksheet. Most likely, Excel will convert the number to scientific notation because it's so large. Next, select the Format-Numbers command, press the Tab key, then type the format as follows: *(###)###-####*. Then press Enter. You might have to expand the column width to see the result. Try formatting 9-digit numbers into social security numbers with the format *###-##-####*

115

Changing the Color of Data

As a final formatting technique, let's examine how to change the color of specific data in the worksheet by customizing an existing format. (Of course, you'll need a color computer system to benefit from this modification.)

To change the color of data, simply type one of the following color codes at the beginning of each section of the desired number format: [black], [white], [red], [green], [blue], [yellow], [magenta], [cyan]. For example, to modify the general format so that all values appear in blue, type

[blue]General

If the format contains two or three parts, enter the color code in front of each part, as in

```
[blue]General;[blue]-General;
```

You can add these color codes to any new or existing format using the procedures described in the previous sections. To change the color of a text entry, you must enter one of the custom formats listed in Table 6-7. (Of course, you can change the color code used in Figure 6-7.)

116

Table 6-7. ***Entering Custom Formats with Color***

You type	Excel displays
General;-General;General;[blue]	Displays numbers in the General format and text in blue
;;;[blue]	Makes all numeric entries invisible and text entries blue
General;-General;;[blue]	Displays positive and negative numbers in the general format, zeros invisible, and text blue
[blue]General;[blue]-General;[blue]General;[blue]	Displays everything in blue

Rounding Numbers

Though Excel can store up to 15 decimal places for a value, many of Excel's built-in number formats round numbers to two decimal places. For example, if you enter the value $45.899 into a cell, Excel displays $45.90. Excel uses a dollar format to display the value with two decimal places and a dollar sign. Remember that the value in the cell has not been changed. The value is merely displayed to look like it has been changed. The cell's actual value is still 45.899, and any references to this cell's value will receive the value 45.899. In short, formatted values are not rounded at all, they only appear to be rounded.

All of Excel's number formats use either two or no decimal places. The exception is the General format, which uses as many places as needed for a value. For example, the two percentage formats are 0% and 0.00%. The first percentage format displays the number with no decimal places and the second displays with two. If you wanted to display percentages with one decimal place, you would have to modify one of the percentage formats. Using the format modification procedures described earlier, you would change one of these formats to read 0.0%. Likewise, you can modify formats to display as many decimal places as you like. If a format has several parts, remember to modify each part.

But if number formats merely display numbers as if they were rounded without really rounding, how do you round numbers so that their values are changed? Well, there are two ways. One way is to tell Excel to round numbers to the values that are displayed. In other words, you can make the number match the display. The value changes for all numbers in the worksheet at one time.

First, use number formats throughout the worksheet to make the numbers appear as you would like them. Then, use the Options-Calculation command and, at the dialog box that appears, press P to check the Precision as Displayed option. Press Enter when finished. Excel warns that your data will *permanently* lose its accuracy before changing the values. If you give the go-ahead, all values throughout the worksheet are changed permanently to match their displayed values.

The second way to round a value does not operate on the entire worksheet at one time. Instead, you can use this method to round a single value in the worksheet. Simply enter the ROUND function into the cell by typing

`=ROUND(value,places)`

In place of the word *value* in the example above, enter whichever value you want rounded. In place of the word *places* enter the number of decimal places to which you want the number rounded. To round the value 34.899 to two places, enter

`=ROUND(34.899,2)`

To round a value produced by a formula, enter the entire formula (without the equal sign) in place of the value. For example, cell A12 might contain the formula =SUM(A1:A10) which produces the value 45.899. To round this value to two places, edit cell A12 and enter

```
=ROUND(SUM(A1:A10),2)
```

Notice that the entire formula without the equal sign is entered in the *value* position. The equal sign is not needed because formulas require them only at the beginning. For more information about the ROUND function and other functions, see Chapter 7.

Changing the Worksheet Display

118

Excel offers several ways to change the overall worksheet display. You might find these changes make your worksheets more attractive. The changes can be made to any worksheet you like without affecting others. One of the most common changes to make to the worksheet view is to remove the gridlines that bound the cells. Your worksheets often can look cleaner without the grids. Another change is to remove the row and column headings that appear at the top and left side of the worksheet. When you are creating a worksheet, these headings are useful for referencing cells. However, if you have finished constructing a worksheet's formulas, you may be able to do without headings. Worksheet display changes are fairly simple and straightforward. First, choose the Options-Display command to reveal the dialog box shown in Figure 6-12.

Now press G to remove the gridlines and/or H to remove the headings. Press Enter when finished. Figure 6-13 shows a worksheet with these elements removed. To replace these elements, repeat the process again.

Adding Borders to Cells

One of the best ways to enhance the appearance of a worksheet is to add borders to the data on the worksheet. Using the Format-Borders command, you can add boxes around cells and ranges,

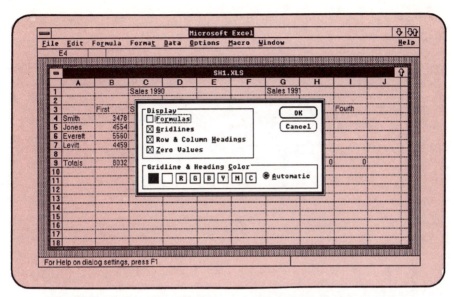

Figure 6-12. **The Options-Display dialog box.**

119

Figure 6-13. **A worksheet with no headings or gridlines.**

and you can add emphasis lines anywhere on the sheet. Figure 6-14 shows a worksheet with various border lines added.

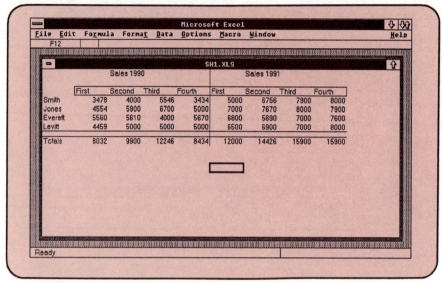

120

*Figure 6-14. **An example worksheet with borders added.***

To add borders to the worksheet, simply highlight the desired cell or range and then select the Format-Borders command. The dialog box in Figure 6-15 appears.

Choose any number of options from the Format-Borders dialog box to add borders to the selected range. Choosing Left adds a border to the left side, choosing Outline adds a border to all sides, and so on. You can combine any number of these options for various results. The Shade option adds shading to the selected range. Figure 6-16 shows the various ways you can add borders.

As shown in Figure 6-16, you can combine border options with row height and column width options to get various effects. Experiment on your worksheets for best results.

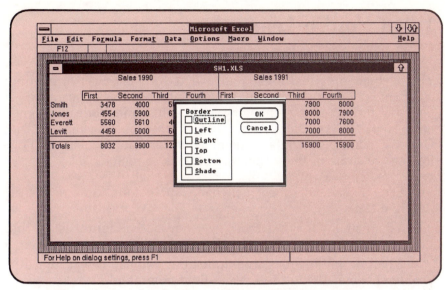

Figure 6-15. *The Format-Borders dialog box.*

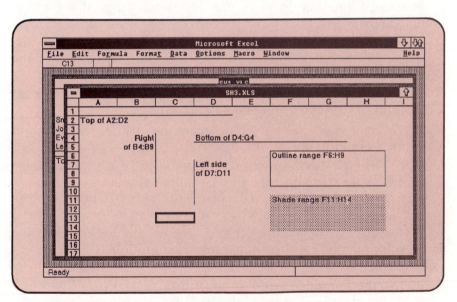

Figure 6-16. *Various border additions.*

What You've Learned

This chapter provided details about Excel's worksheet formatting commands. These commands let you enhance the appearance of data on the sheet by changing type fonts and styles. Various options in the Format menu provide these enhancements. The Options menu also contains commands for data formatting. Following are some of the formatting options to remember:

- ▶ Each Excel worksheet can have up to four fonts active at one time.
- ▶ You can switch between the four active fonts using the commands Ctrl-1, Ctrl-2, Ctrl-3 and Ctrl-4.
- ▶ Excel provides four active fonts, but you can select four different ones using the Format-Font command.
- ▶ Align information in a cell with the Format-Alignment command.
- ▶ Excel's number formats are accessible from the Format-Numbers listing.
- ▶ Some formats appear to round numbers, but they just display rounded numbers without rounding the value of the data.
- ▶ You can hide zero values using a modified number format or the Options-Display command.
- ▶ You can make data invisible using the custom format ;;; in the Format-Numbers dialog box.
- ▶ Use the ROUND function to permanently round numbers off. Alternatively, use the Options-Calculation command with the Precision as Displayed option to round numbers throughout the worksheet.
- ▶ To remove the gridlines that appear on the worksheet or the column and row headings, use the Options-Display command.
- ▶ Use the Format-Borders command to add borders, lines and boxes to various areas of the worksheet. This command will also provide shading for selected areas.

Chapter 7

More About Functions

In This Chapter

▶ *How functions work*
▶ *Arguments*
▶ *Excel's most important functions*

Excel's functions are an important part of worksheet operations. You'll find that functions expand your worksheet capabilities significantly. This chapter shows you the Excel functions that you might use most often. You'll also learn some basic rules about entering functions and arguments.

How Functions Work

As mentioned in a previous chapter, functions perform special calculations for your worksheets. But to use functions, you must enter them properly. Functions are divided into three basic parts, the function name, the parentheses and the arguments, as follows:

    SUM(A1:A5,10,A3 + 4)

All functions must be entered into cells or formulas using all three parts. If the function is the only thing in cell (as often is the case), then it should be entered as a formula by including the = sign in front of it. The parentheses are the same for all functions. Parentheses hold the arguments and come directly after the function name. The function name reminds you of the function's purpose.

Arguments

The arguments differ greatly from function to function. Arguments are the values on which a function operates. Arguments can be constant values, as in SUM(5,10). They can be cell references, as in SUM(A5,C3,G6). They can be range references, as in SUM(A1:A10). They can be formulas, as in SUM(A1+35). And they can be other functions, as in SUM(A5,SUM(A1:A10)). Other special arguments are also used. A particular function may not allow all argument types. The syntax of the function determines which types of arguments it takes. (By the way, the SUM function happens to accept all these types of arguments, which is why it's used in this chapter as an example.)

One of the helpful features of range references in formulas is that they expand and contract to accommodate changes to the worksheet. Suppose that you enter a formula into cell B10 that adds the range B1:B8 using the function =SUM(B1:B8). Later, you decide to insert a row above row 3. This expands the range to B1:B9 in order to cover the same data. Excel automatically changes the range reference in the formula. Likewise, when you delete, copy or move information, Excel adjusts the cell or range references. Range arguments are also useful because you may only enter 14 arguments per function.

Excel's Most Important Functions

Excel offers dozens of special functions for many purposes. You will probably not need to learn them all. But there are some functions that you should know a little about. These are the functions you'll use most in your applications. This section discusses the most important Excel functions, providing examples of their use.

Summing Columns and Rows (SUM)

You've already seen how the SUM function works. It's used to add the values in a group of cells. This group can be either a range of cells or a list of references, as in the following examples:

```
=SUM(A1:A10)
=SUM(A1,A2,A6,B4,B9,C32)
```

Notice that the list can include cells that are not adjacent to one another. This is the advantage of using a list. Any of the references in the list can be an expression itself, as in the following example:

125

```
=SUM(A1,A4,C5+10,R22)
```

The third reference in the list is the expression *C5+10*. If any of the cells in the range or list are blank or contain text, Excel treats them as zeros.

Calculating an Average (AVERAGE)

The AVERAGE function is used to calculate the mean average of a group of numbers. Although you could accomplish this task with basic worksheet formulas, the AVERAGE function makes it easy. Often, the numbers being averaged will fall in a row or a column, but you can also average randomly plotted values. Hence, a range reference or list of references can be used as the argument, as follows:

```
AVERAGE(A1:A10)
AVERAGE(A1,C3,B25,G10)
```

The first example is a range of cells. You can use any valid worksheet range, including a block of cells. The second example is a group of cells placed at various spots in the worksheet. As in most functions, you can substitute constant values, calculations or other functions as the arguments.

Keep in mind that including zero values inadvertently in the argument may destroy the accuracy of an average. When used with a range reference, the AVERAGE function ignores text entries and blank cells. Hence, when you use a range as the argument, it's okay if some of the cells in that range are blank or contain text. If you use the AVERAGE function with a list of cells, the function interprets text *and blank cells* as values of zero. So be careful not to use a reference to a cell that is either blank or text.

Using Worksheet Logic (IF)

126 The IF function is perhaps the most powerful and useful of all worksheet functions. It provides most of the logic you'll need for evaluating information. The IF function uses *conditions*, or tests regarding the value of a cell. For example, a condition might test if the value of A1 equals 100. The value of A1 is either 100 or not. Hence, the condition answer is either true or false. If the condition proves true, one value is returned. If the condition proves false, another value is returned. A simple logical statement can be the basis of some powerful operations. Logic lets your worksheets perform different actions based on different values.

A condition must use a logical operator to create a test. Excel offers several logical operators, as listed:

>	is greater than
<	is less than
=	is equal to
>=	is greater than or equal to
<=	is less than or equal to
<>	is not equal to

With that, here's an example of the IF function at work. This function might be placed in cell A4:

=IF(A1=100,"Must be less than 100",A1*2)

This function says, if the value of A1 is equal to 100, then place the message "Must be less than 100" in cell A4, otherwise calculate the value of A1*2. The function requires that the arguments be entered in this order: first the condition followed by a comma, then the *value if true* followed by a comma, then the *value if false.*

The value if true and the value if false can be any constant value, text string, cell reference or formula. Notice that this example uses a text string for the value if true and a formula for the value if false. If you use text as one of these values, it must be surrounded by quotation marks as shown in the example. Figure 7-1 shows what the previous example might look like on the screen.

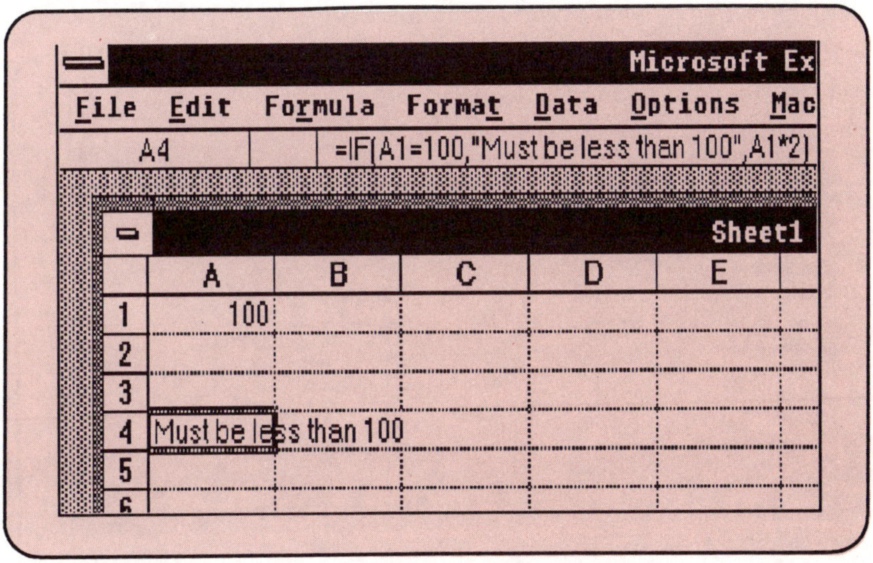

Figure 7-1. Example of the IF function.

You can enter different values into cell A1. If you enter 100, the message appears in cell A4. If you enter anything else, cell A4 contains the value of that number times two.

In the previous example, you might substitute => for = in the condition. The function would read

=IF(A1=>100,"Must be less than 100",A1*2)

This way, any value equal to or greater than 100 will produce the message.

Looking Up a Value in a Table (VLOOKUP)

The VLOOKUP function tries to match a value with a another set of values contained in a table, and returns one of the values when the match is made. The value that you are trying to find in the table is called the *lookup value*. For example, you might have a table of prices for merchandise and want to search that table for item number 125. When item number 125 is located in the table, the price of the item is returned. Figure 7-2 shows an example.

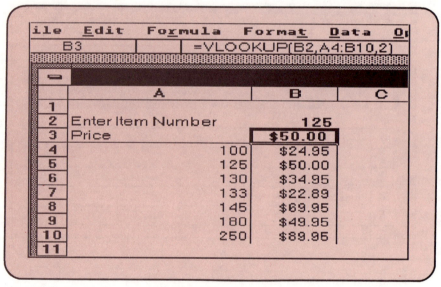

Figure 7-2. A simple lookup table.

The VLOOKUP function searches vertically in a column of values, then returns a corresponding value from the another table column. The function works like this:

= VLOOKUP(value,table range,offset)

The lookup function in Figure 7-2 was entered into cell B3 as follows:

```
=VLOOKUP(B2,A4:B10,2)
```

The value is the number or text in the first column of the table that you are trying to match with corresponding information. This can be any number, text, cell reference or formula. For the Figure 7-2 example, the value was entered as the cell reference B2 so any number entered into cell B2 becomes the value for the lookup. The *table range* is the worksheet range containing the table. The first column of this range, called the *lookup column*, should include the list of values for which you will be searching. The table can then include as many more columns as necessary to contain all information. Additional columns are called *offset* columns, and they contain the cells with information you want to return when you select a value from the lookup column. When entering the VLOOKUP formula, the lookup column is referred to as offset 1, the next column is offset 2, and so on. The example in Figure 7-2 shows only one offset column.

When the function finds the lookup value in the lookup column, it remembers the row position of the lookup value. Then the function searches across the table to return information from the column specified by the offset value listed in the formula. Figure 7-3 shows how Figure 7-2 looks with more offset columns. The lookup formulas in cells B3, C3 and D3 return information from each of the columns of the table, using the following functions:

```
=VLOOKUP(B2,A4:D10,2)
=VLOOKUP(B2,A4:D10,3)
=VLOOKUP(B2,A4:D10,4)
```

Notice that the formulas are identical, except that they contain different offset values, selecting values from different columns along one row of the table.

When you create lookup tables and the lookup formulas that use them, keep some basic rules in mind. First, the values in the lookup column must be in ascending order (sorted), as they are in Figure 7-3. If the values are text, they must be in alphabetical order. If the lookup column is not in ascending order, the function may return incorrect values. Excel searches the lookup column until it finds a direct match. If a direct match cannot be found the closest value smaller than the search variable is used. Therefore, if a lookup value is greater than all values in the table, the last value in the table is used because it's

129

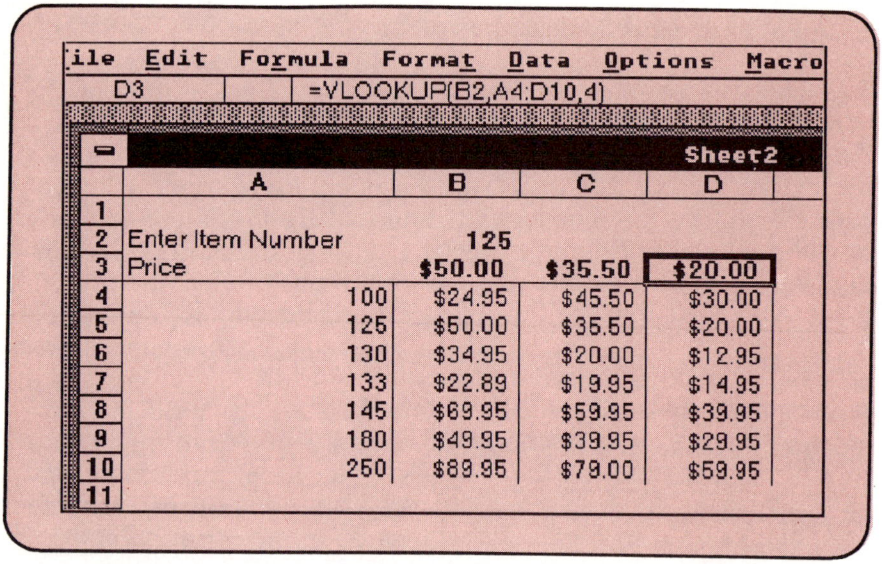

	A	B	C	D
	ile Edit Formula Format Data Options Macro			
	D3	=VLOOKUP(B2,A4:D10,4)		
				Sheet2
1				
2	Enter Item Number	125		
3	Price	$50.00	$35.50	$20.00
4	100	$24.95	$45.50	$30.00
5	125	$50.00	$35.50	$20.00
6	130	$34.95	$20.00	$12.95
7	133	$22.89	$19.95	$14.95
8	145	$69.95	$59.95	$39.95
9	180	$49.95	$39.95	$29.95
10	250	$89.95	$79.00	$59.95
11				

130

Figure 7-3. An extended table with three offset columns.

the largest. If the lookup value is smaller than all values in the table, then the function returns the error: #VALUE!

If the lookup column contains text, then the lookup function must be able to match the lookup value exactly, including upper- and lower-case letters. When no match is found the function will return the error: #VALUE! Even if the lookup column contains text, the offset columns can contain numeric values or text.

Rounding Numbers (ROUND)

The ROUND function rounds a value to a specified number of places. The difference between using this function the number formats that round numbers is that the ROUND function permanently changes the number to the rounded value. If you reference a cell with a rounded value in a formula, the rounded value is used. Using the Format-Number command merely displays a number with a certain number of decimal places rather than changing the number. References to numbers rounded with Format-Number use the actual, unrounded value. An example of the ROUND function follows:

=ROUND(C3,2)

This function rounds the value in cell C3 to two decimal places. Enter the desired cell or range as the first argument, then enter a comma and the number of decimal places desired.

Entering the Current Date and Time (NOW)

Excel includes a special function, NOW, that gets the current date and time from your system clock (if available) or from the DOS startup date and time. To use NOW, just enter

=NOW()

Notice that the function has no arguments, but that the parentheses are still included. You can use the NOW function in date-oriented calculations. For example, you can determine how many days have elapsed since a particular date by using the formula: =NOW()-A1. Enter any date into cell A1, and the formula calculates the difference between the current date and the date you entered. The date you enter should be a past date.

131

If you use NOW by itself, you should format the result of the formula to any valid date or time format using the Format-Number command.

Loan Calculations

Excel provides a number of functions for calculating loan amounts. There are four parts of a loan: the *principal amount, periodic interest rate, periodic payment* and *number of payments* (or term). These might be entered into a worksheet as shown in Figure 7-4.

The purpose of the worksheet is to calculate any one of these amounts when you know the other three. For example, you can calculate the monthly payment amount when you know the principal, interest rate and term. Following are the Excel functions for calculating the interest, payment or term of a loan:

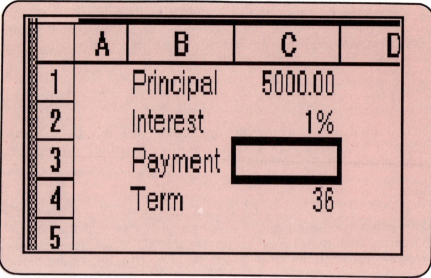

Figure 7-4. **The beginning of a loan calculation worksheet.**

PMT(rate,term,principal)	Calculates the periodic payment when you enter the interest rate, term and principal as arguments.
NPER(rate,payment,principal)	Calculates the term when you enter the interest rate, periodic payment and principal amounts as arguments.
RATE(term,payment,principal)	Calculates the interest rate when you enter the term, payment and principal as arguments.

Suppose you wanted to calculate the monthly payment amount using the worksheet from Figure 7-4. Simply enter the formula =PMT(C2,C4,C1) into cell C3 as shown in Figure 7-5. In this case, you would enter values for the principal, interest rate and term only.

Note that the interest rate is entered as the periodic rate. This periodic rate should be for the same time periods entered in

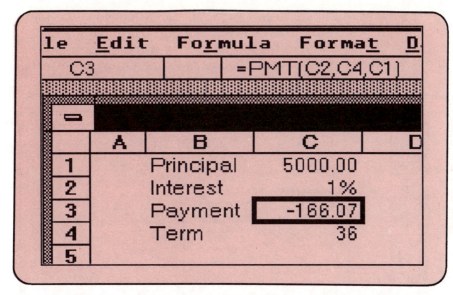

Figure 7-5. Example of calculating the principal of a loan.

133

the term. In the example, the term is 36 months, so you should enter the monthly interest rate. If you know only the annual interest rate, simply divide the annual rate by 12 to get the monthly rate. Or you can enter the formula =12% / 12 to calculate the periodic rate from the annual rate.

Another thing to notice is that the payment amount appears as a negative because it represents cash out. When using sums you have borrowed, the principal is positive (cash in) and the payment is negative (cash out). For sums loaned, the principal is negative and the payment is positive.

The next step of this worksheet example is to calculate the amount of interest and principal paid at each payment. As you might already know, you pay more interest at the beginning of a loan than at the end. The proportion of interest to principal is different for each payment. Using the PPMT function, you can determine how much principal is being paid with each payment. This function uses the following arguments:

=PPMT(rate,payment number,term,principal)

Given the rate, term, and principal, PPMT calculates the principal payment for any given payment number. First, enter the payment numbers from 1 to 36 (or whatever the term requires) down column B as shown in Figure 7-6. Figure 7-6 also shows some basic formatting applied to the worksheet, including the border around the table of values and some number formats.

	A	B	C	D	E
1		Principal	5000.00		
2		Interest	1%		
3		Payment	-166.07		
4		Term	36		
5					
6		Amounts Paid			
7		on Each Payment			
8		Payment	Principal	Interest	
9		1			
10		2			
11		3			
12		4			
13		5			
14		6			
15		7			
16		8			
17		9			
18		10			

Figure 7-6.   Enter the payment numbers on the worksheet.

The next step is to create the first formula. This will calculate the interest paid at the first payment. Enter the formula in cell C9 as follows:

=PPMT($C$2,B9,$C$4,$C$1)

Notice that all the references are absolute except the payment number, which will be copied down column C to produce each payment. But first, enter the formula for the interest amount in cell D9 as follows:

=$C$3-C9

This simply takes the payment amount and subtracts the PPMT amount for each payment number. You can see that the first payment consists of $116.07 of principal and $50.00 of interest. To view the remaining payments, highlight the range C9:D44, then select the Edit-Fill Down command. The result should look something like Figure 7-7.

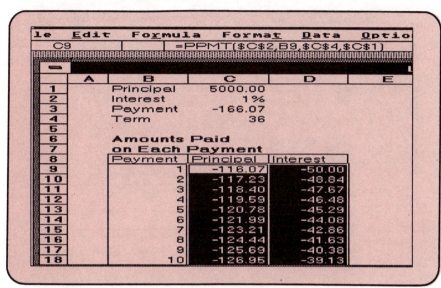

Figure 7-7.   Completing the payment formulas.

The final step is to use the SUM function to total each column at the bottom. Then, add the two totals for the entire amount of the loan, including principal and interest. The totals are shown in Figure 7-8.

What You've Learned

This chapter provided details about some important Excel functions. You'll find these functions most useful in your worksheets. But remember, Excel has dozens more, some of which are listed in Appendix A. Consult the *Excel Functions and Macros* guide for a complete listing. Following are some important points covered in this chapter:

▶ Functions consist of three main parts: the function name, the parentheses and the arguments.

▶ Different functions allow different kinds of arguments.

135

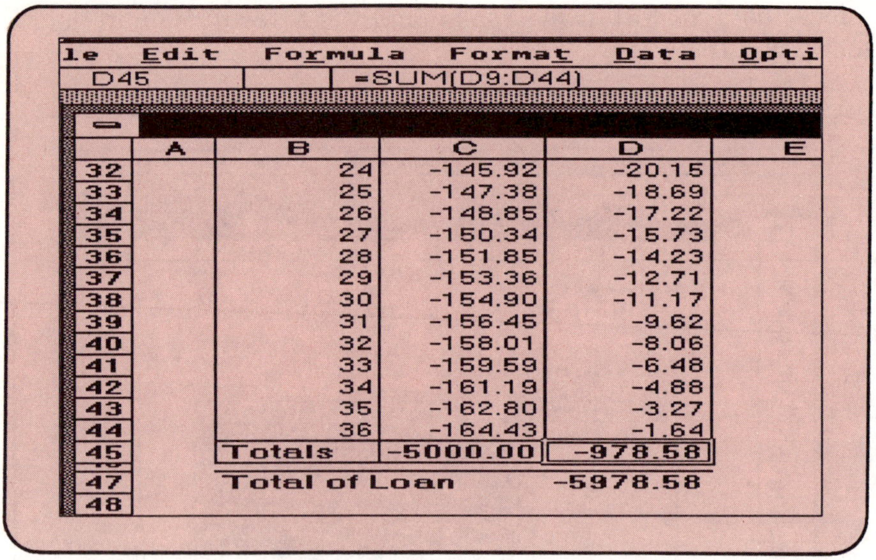
le Edit Formula Format Data Opti
D45 =SUM(D9:D44)
A B C D E
32 24 -145.92 -20.15
33 25 -147.38 -18.69
34 26 -148.85 -17.22
35 27 -150.34 -15.73
36 28 -151.85 -14.23
37 29 -153.36 -12.71
38 30 -154.90 -11.17
39 31 -156.45 -9.62
40 32 -158.01 -8.06
41 33 -159.59 -6.48
42 34 -161.19 -4.88
43 35 -162.80 -3.27
44 36 -164.43 -1.64
45 Totals -5000.00 -978.58
47 Total of Loan -5978.58
48

Figure 7-8. Adding totals.

- Use the SUM function to add rows, columns or any list of cells.
- Use the AVERAGE function to calculate the mean average of a group of values.
- The IF function lets you perform two different actions based on the result of a test. The test consists of a TRUE/FALSE condition.
- To look up a value in a table, use the VLOOKUP function.
- Use ROUND to round numbers to a chosen number of decimal places.
- The NOW function enters the current date and time into the cell.
- Excel includes a set of loan-oriented functions that calculate the rate, term, payment and principal of a loan.

Chapter 8

Printing the Worksheet

In This Chapter

137

- ▶ *Overview of printing*
- ▶ *Adding and removing printers*
- ▶ *Changing printer connections*
- ▶ *Setting up your printer*
- ▶ *A basic printout*
- ▶ *Enhancing the printout*
- ▶ *Printing column titles*

Printing is an indispensable function for any program. In Excel, you can print your worksheets using a basic printing procedure, or you can enhance the printout using several print options. This chapter shows you how to print your worksheets using Excel's basic printing capabilities. Plus, you'll learn how to enhance the printout for special needs by adding page numbers, headers, footers and more.

Overview of Printing

Excel's basic printing process is fairly simple. Start by using the File-Printer Setup command to specify details about your printer. You can confirm that you installed the right printer and connected it correctly, or switch to another printer.

Next, set up the format for your printout. Tell Excel what part of the worksheet you want to print with the Options-Set Print Area command. Add headers, footers and page numbers, or change page margins, using the File-Page Setup command. For long lists and tables, you might want to print column headings at the top of each page using the Options-Set Print Titles command. Finally, print the worksheet with the File-Print command.

138 This is the basic printing procedure discussed in this chapter. You might want to try out the steps listed throughout the chapter on a sample worksheet.

Giving Excel Access to Your Printer

When you installed Excel, you specified the printer you have and connected it to a printer port. You had the opportunity to select several printers during installation. Before you try to print a worksheet, take a look at the printers that are currently available to Excel and double-check that your printer is on the list. Select the File-Printer Setup command to view the list of available printers, as shown in Figure 8-1.

If installed correctly, your printer should appear in this list (it might be the only printer in the list). Along with the printer name, the listing should show the port to which it is connected, as in HP DeskJet PLUS on LPT 1. If the listing is correct, you can skip the next section of this chapter and jump right to the section titled *Setting Up Your Printer*.

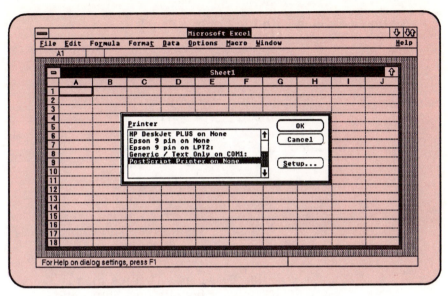

Figure 8-1.   The Printer Setup list.

139

Adding a Printer

It's possible that your printer is not shown on the printer setup list or that the printer port is incorrect. Perhaps you selected the wrong printer during the installation, or maybe you have changed printers since you installed Excel. Whatever the case, you have two ways to get your printer (or printers) on the list: either reinstall Excel as described in Chapter 1 and make the printer selections over again, or use the *Control Panel* to place your printer on the list without reinstalling the program.

As you may have guessed, using the Control Panel is the easiest of the two methods. Plus, you can use the Control Panel any time you like, and you can use it repeatedly, switching and adding printers as you heart desires. If you need to add your printer to the Printer Setup list, follow these Quick Steps:

Adding a Printer with the Control Panel

1. Press Alt-Space.

   Invokes the Control menu for Excel.

2. Select the Run option by pressing U. If you have a mouse, simply click on the control menu icon for the program and select the Run option.

   The dialog box shown in Figure 8-2 will appear on the screen.

3. Press P to select the Control Panel option, then press Enter.

   The Control Panel appears on screen as shown in Figure 8-3. The Control Panel shows you the current date and time and contains three menus: Installation, Setup and Preferences.

140

4. Press Alt-I to select the Installation menu, then choose the Add New Printer option.

   Excel now asks you to insert a disk into drive A. Locate your original Excel Utilities disk, insert it in drive A and press Enter. Excel soon displays a list of printers.

5. Choose your printer from the list and press Enter. Press Enter again when Excel presents the next dialog box.

   This copies the selected printer file to the Windows directory, where your other Excel program files are located. When finished, you will be returned to the Control Panel.

6. Press Alt-Space, then C to close the Control Panel.

   The printer you selected is now available for your printouts. □

To check that the printer is now available, use the File-Printer Setup command to view the list of available printers. The printer you added should now appear in this list. If you need to add another printer at any time, repeat the steps just listed.

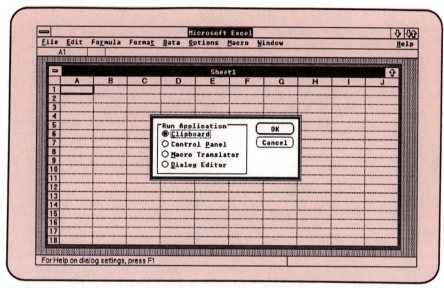

Figure 8-2. **The Run options from the Control menu.**

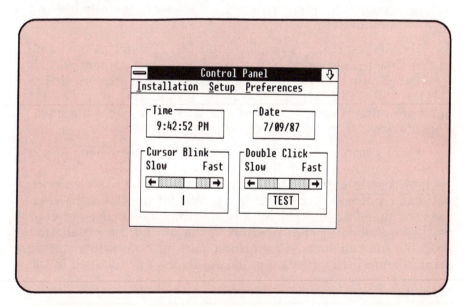

Figure 8-3. **The Control Panel.**

> ▶ **Tip:** Some memory-resident programs prohibit you from using Excel's Control Panel due to memory conflicts. If this is the case, you might have to run Excel without using these memory-resident programs, which could mean changing your AUTOEXEC.BAT file so that the programs do not automatically load into memory when you start the computer. Check a DOS manual for more information about these concerns.

Changing Printer Connections

142

Printers are connected to the computer by means of cables that are plugged into *ports*. A port allows your computer to output information to other devices such as a printer or modem. There are two main types of ports: communication ports (called COMM ports), which are always *serial*; and printer ports (called LPT ports), which may be serial or *parallel*. Generally, when you purchase your computer hardware, you specify the number and type of ports desired.

Usually, a printer is connected to LPT1, which is the name of the first printer port. If you have a second printer port, it would be called LPT2. You can also connect printers to the COMM ports: COMM1, COMM2 and so on. However, COMM ports are often reserved for modems and other telecommunications devices.

Excel's Printer Setup list specified the port to which each printer is connected (or the port to which it *should* be connected). You might need to connect a printer to a different port, particularly if you just added the printer to the list. Other reasons for changing the port for a printer include changes in your hardware system or simply errors made during the installation process. You can specify the printer port for each printer in the Printer Setup list by using the Control Panel, as explained in the following Quick Steps.

Q Changing a Printer's Port Specification

1. Press Alt-Space.

   Invokes the Control menu.

2. Press U to select the Run option. If you have a mouse, simply click on the control menu icon and select the Run option.

   The dialog box shown in Figure 8-2 appears.

3. Press P to select the Control Panel option, then press Enter.

   The Control Panel appears on screen as shown in Figure 8-3.

4. Press Alt-S to invoke the Setup menu, then press Enter to select the Connections option.

   Excel displays its list of available printers and a list of available ports.

143

5. Select the printer whose port specification you want to change by using the ↓ key to highlight its name in the list.

6. Press Tab, then use the ↑ and ↓ keys to highlight the new port for the printer. Press Enter when finished.

   □

Excel does not allow two printers to be connected to the same port at the same time. All printers that are not actually connected should get the port designation none. You can, of course, change a printer's port at any time. Be sure to connect serial printers to serial ports and parallel printers to parallel ports. Check your printer manual to determine whether you have a serial or parallel printer. If you have a serial printer, you should make sure the Communications Settings in Excel's Control Panel match the printer's settings. With the Control Panel on the screen, press Alt-S to choose the Setup option. Next, press M to select the Communications Settings option. There are options for Baud Rate, Word Length, Parity, Stop Bits, Handshake and

Port. Refer to your printer manual for the appropriate settings for all options but the Port option. After making the desired changes, press Enter.

Setting Up Your Printer

The first time you use your printer with Excel, you should check the Setup options. Excel can take advantage of the options and capabilities that are available with each printer. Often, you have to provide more details about your printer so Excel knows the capabilities available.

To view the Setup options for your printer, select the File-Setup command and then highlight the name of your printer in the list. Finally, press Alt-S to see the Setup options for the printer you highlighted. Figure 8-4 shows the Setup options for the HP DeskJet Family. When your printer is part of a family of printers, you need to specify the exact model of printer that you are using. Other options you can select include paper sizes, paper orientation, resolution and paper type (or source).

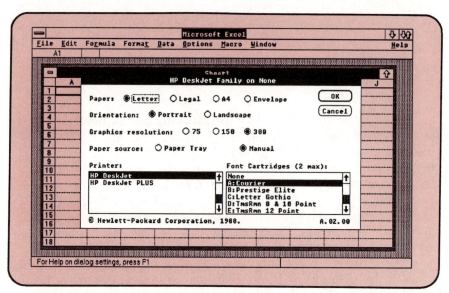

Figure 8-4.   Example Setup options screen for HP DeskJet printers.

Select the correct options. (Your Setup screen may look different than the one shown in Figure 8-4.) Press Enter when finished, then press Esc to return to the Excel worksheet. You are now ready to print.

Basic Printing

Once your printer is properly installed, connected and set up, and it appears correctly in the Printer Setup list, you are ready to begin printing. First, select the File-Print command to get the dialog box shown in Figure 8-5.

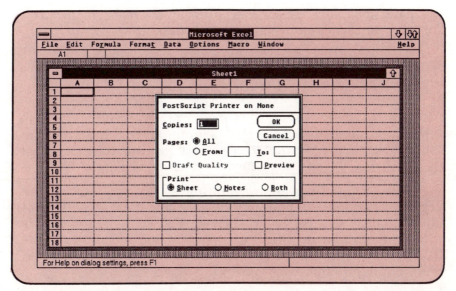

Figure 8-5.   The Print dialog box.

The Print dialog box contains a few choices you can make before printing. Following is a list of these options.

Copies   You can print multiple copies of each page with this option. Just enter the number of copies you would like to print in the space provided.

Pages	This option lets you select the page(s) you want to print. You can specify the range or indicate that you want to print all pages.
Draft Quality	This option is available for most dot matrix printers. It lets you print at a reduced quality for faster performance. This option prints the worksheet data using the printer's built-in font, which is often less attractive than printing without the Draft option selected.
Preview	This option causes the printout to appear on the screen so you can examine it before printing.
Print	Select Sheet to print the worksheet, Notes to print the notes attached to the worksheet cells, or Both to print both.

146 After making your choices, press Enter to begin printing. Press Esc to cancel and return to the worksheet.

Previewing the Printout

With Excel, you can view each page prior to printing. To preview the printout, select the Preview option from the File-Print dialog box, then press Enter. The first page of the worksheet appears in a reduced image on the screen as in Figure 8-6.

If the printout consists of multiple pages, you can use the Next and Previous buttons to flip back and forth. The Cancel button returns you to the worksheet. The Print button begins printing to the printer directly from the preview screen. The Zoom button enlarges the preview to its actual size so you can examine the printout more closely.

If you have a mouse, you can enlarge the preview by clicking on the area of the page that you would like to view more closely.

Page Breaks

If your worksheet is too large to fit onto one page, Excel splits the work onto two or more pages. Excel makes the split based on

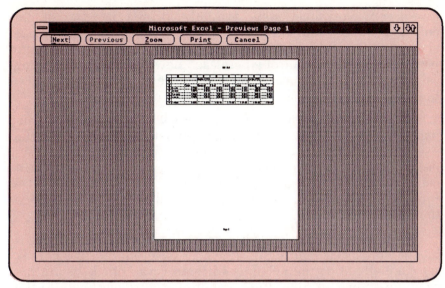

Figure 8-6.   Example of the print preview feature.

147

your current page dimensions, margin settings and cell widths. Excel always splits the worksheet at the beginning of a column (vertically) and/or row (horizontally), so the information in a cell will never be split between two pages.

If the automatic page breaks are not adequate for your worksheet, there are many ways to make adjustments:

► Change the page margins using the File-Page Setup command, as explained later in this chapter.

► Change the page orientation to Landscape to print the worksheet sideways on the paper. You can choose the Landscape orientation with the File-Page Setup command, also described later in this chapter.

► If the worksheet is too wide, decrease the widths of some cells if possible.

► Remove the row and column headings that print with the data, as explained later in the chapter. This won't add much space, but sometimes a little bit is all you need.

► If your printer has a scaling feature, use it to shrink the page when you print. The scaling feature, if available, appears in the File-Printer Setup options. See *Setting Up Your Printer* earlier in this chapter for more details.

If your worksheet is still too large for one page, you might consider adding your own page breaks to override page breaks chosen by Excel. The worksheet will still print on two or more pages, but you can control where each new page begins. As long as each page fits into the prescribed page size and margin settings, you can set a page break anywhere on the worksheet.

There are three ways to set page breaks. First, you can establish the right-hand side of each page, letting Excel break the pages at the bottom. Simply move the cell pointer to the column designating the right side of the first page, move to the top-most cell in that column (row 1), then choose the Options-Set Page Break command. The page breaks to the left of the column where the cursor is located.

148

You can continue to set breaks for the right side of all pages in the worksheet. Figure 8-7 shows an example of a page break set manually at column H and indicated by a dotted line. In the example shown in Figure 8-7, columns A through G are to the left of the manual page break and will print on one page. However, unless another page break is specified in the worksheet, all pages to the right of column H are determined by Excel.

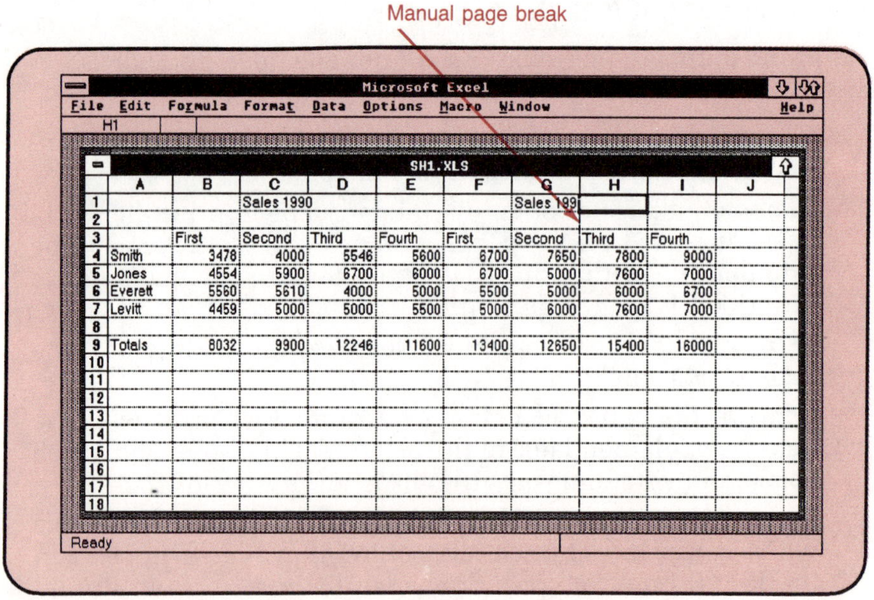

Manual page break

Figure 8-7.   *Setting a page break manually.*

You can also set the bottom of a page by moving the pointer to column A of the row just below the last row you want to include in the page. For example, to break the page at row 45, place the pointer in cell A46. Next, select the Options-Set Page Break command.

Finally, you can set both the bottom and right side of a page by selecting the cell below and to the right of the bottom-right corner of the page. For example, to set the right side of a page at column G and the bottom at row 45, select cell H46. Then choose the Options-Set Page Break command. This technique affects only pages above and to the left of the cell you selected (to the left of column H and above row 45 in our example). For other areas of the worksheet, you must set additional page breaks or Excel will break the pages automatically.

Page breaks remain active until you remove them. Establishing new page breaks does not alter existing breaks, it simply adds to them. To remove a page break, reselect the column, row or cell that was used to create the break and choose the Options-Remove Page Break command. This command appears only when the pointer is in the correct cell, row or column.

149

> ▶ **Tip:** Excel usually prints non-contiguous sections of text on separate sheets. To print non-contiguous sections on the same sheet, use the Format-Column Width command to eliminate the unused or unwanted space between two areas of data. Simply enter a value of 0 for the columns to be eliminated. By modifying the worksheet in this way, you collapse it so that it fits on one page.

Selecting a Print Area

You will probably find the need to print specific sections of a worksheet, such as a range of cells. Although you can set the right and bottom page breaks to include the area you want to print, it's easier to single out the area as a separate page and then print that page. Highlight the range you want to print, then select the Options-Set Print Area command. When you select the File-Print command, Excel will print only the established print area. If the area is too large to fit onto one page, Excel will break it into multiple pages.

You can highlight multiple ranges as the print area and Excel will print all the ranges at one time, each range on a separate page. Highlighting multiple ranges was discussed in Chapter 5. With all the ranges highlighted, choose the Options-Set Print Area command, then print the worksheet. Each range will appear on a separate page in the order in which they were selected.

To remove the established print area, use the Formula-Define Name command to show all established range name on the worksheet. If a print area is set, the name Print_Area appears in the name list. (Excel automatically applies this name to the currently selected print area.) Select this name and press Alt-D to delete it. You can now establish manual page breaks or set a new print area.

150 Enhancing the Printout with File-Page Setup

There are many parts of the basic printout that you might want to change. For instance, Excel automatically prints the worksheet gridlines along with the data. Many people like to remove gridlines for the printout. The column and row headings are another automatic addition that you might want to remove. In addition to giving you these two options, Excel adds a header and footer to the basic printout. The header consists of the name of the worksheet and the footer is the page number.

The File-Page Setup command controls print enhancements. Take a look at these controls by selecting the File-Page Setup command. The dialog box shown in Figure 8-8 appears.

The following list includes each File-Page Setup option and its purpose.

Header

This option adds a header to the top of each page in the printout. You can include any text plus special commands to control the appearance of the header. See *Adding Headers and Footers* later in this chapter for more details.

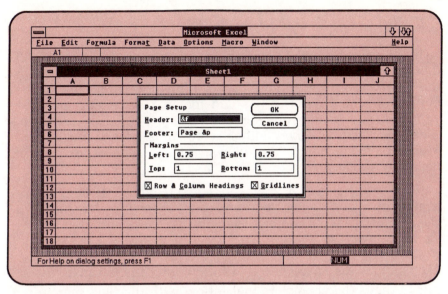

Figure 8-8.   The File-Page Setup options.

151

Footer	This option adds a footer to the bottom of each page.
Margins	Margin measurements control the top, bottom, left and right margins of the page. Excel will include information with the next page if it does not fit within the specified margins. Margins are relative to the paper size currently set with the Printer Setup options.
Row and Column Headings	This option prints or suppresses the column headings for your worksheet printout.
Print Gridlines	This option prints or suppresses the cell gridlines on the worksheet printout only. The Print Gridlines option has no connection with the Options-Display command, which affects the gridlines for the screen display.

Make the appropriate selections for the printout, then press Enter to accept your options. When you print the worksheet, your changes will be effective. Remember that the Gridlines option and the Row and Column Headings option affect the printout only, not the screen display.

Adding Headers and Footers

Using the Header and Footer options, you can add headers and footers to your printouts. A *header* is a line of text repeated at the top of each page, and a *footer* is a line of text repeated at the bottom of each page. Headers and footers can contain any text you like, plus commands for automatically entering the date, time and page number. Other commands placed inside the header or footer control the placement and style of text in the header or footer.

To define a header and/or footer, select the File-Page Setup command. Then, enter text and any special codes into the Header space and/or Footer space. Special codes and their effects are as follows:

&L	Aligns the characters that follow with the left margin
&R	Aligns the characters that follow with the right margin
&C	Centers the characters that follow
&P	Prints the page number
&D	Prints the current date in the format 2/24/91
&T	Prints the current time in the format 1:30:00 PM
&F	Prints the current file name
&B	Boldface
&I	Italics

The commands &L, &R and &C align information in the header and footer. You can use one of these codes to align the entire header or footer or combine the codes to break up the header or footer into sections. Figure 8-9 shows some footer examples.

Printing Column Headings

Worksheets are often set up with a row of titles or column headings above the columns of data to clarify what information is in each column. If the columns contain many rows of data, your printout might be several pages long, and you might want the col-

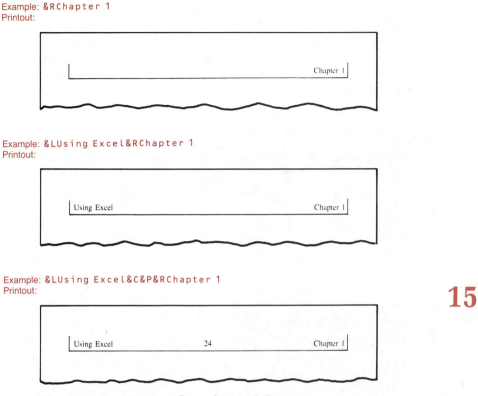

Example: &RChapter 1
Printout:

Example: &LUsing Excel&RChapter 1
Printout:

Example: &LUsing Excel&C&P&RChapter 1
Printout:

Figure 8-9.   Examples of Excel footers.

umn headings to print at the top of each page. While a header is a useful label for each page, you cannot align headers with work-sheet columns. Stick to using the header to print the document name, the date and other such information.

Excel can automatically print column headings at the top of each page and align the headings with the columns in the work-sheet. All you have to do is specify which cells (probably a row or two near the top of the worksheet) contain the column head-ings. First highlight the entire row (or rows) containing the col-umn headings, then use the Options-Set Print Titles command. The selected rows are now set as the print column headings.

Suppose you wanted to print the worksheet shown in Fig-ure 8-10 with the column headings at the top of each printed page. First, highlight the entire block of data that you want to print without including the headings. Use the Options-Set Print Area command to set this block as the current print area. Next, highlight the row containing the headings (row 3 in Figure 8-10) and use the Options-Set Print Titles command. (Remember, you can highlight a row using Shift-Space.) Finally, print the worksheet normally with the File-Print command. The column headings you selected (such as Title, Author, Call No, Subj and Date Pub in Figure 8-10) will print above the appropriate column on each page.

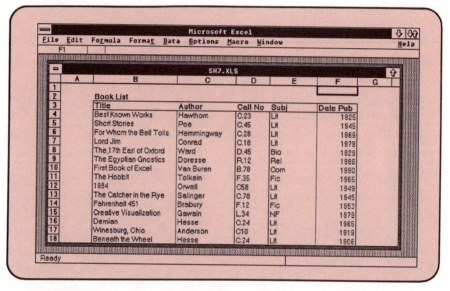

Figure 8-10.   Worksheet with column headings.

To remove the print titles you've established, select the Format-Define Name command and remove the name Print_Titles from the list.

What You've Learned

This chapter provided details about printing worksheets. The chapter explained how to use the File-Printer Setup command to select a printer and its port, and showed you how to add a printer or alter printer port connections using the Excel Control Panel. The chapter also discussed printing a worksheet with the File-Print command and making various enhancements to the output using the File-Page Setup options. Following is a list of things to remember:

▶ When you installed Excel, you specified your printer and its connection port. You can modify these settings using the Control Panel.

▶ The File-Printer Setup command gives you a list of available printers and each printer's connection.

▶ You can have as many printers as you like active in the Printer Setup list. Just add new printers with the Control Panel.

▶ The Control Panel is also used to specify the connection ports for printers. A port can have only one printer assigned to it at one time.

▶ The first time you use a printer in Excel, you should use the File-Printer Setup command to specify details about the printer.

155

▶ You can preview a printout on screen using the Preview option in the File-Print command.

▶ Excel automatically breaks pages for the printout unless you manually set page breaks with the Options-Set Page Break command.

▶ To print a specific area of the worksheet, use the Options-Set Print Area command.

▶ You can remove the printout gridlines, column headings and row headings using the File-Page Setup options.

▶ You can change or remove the page header and footer using the File-Page Setup options.

▶ By selecting cells containing column headings and then using the Options-Set Print Titles command, you can print column headings on each page.

Chapter 9

Charting Your Data

In This Chapter

▶ *Parts of a chart*
▶ *Charting your worksheet data*
▶ *Changing the chart type*
▶ *Modifying the chart*
▶ *Creating combination charts*

This chapter provides complete instructions for creating charts in Excel. First, it gives you a brief overview of the charting process. After this, the chapter explains some basic charting terminology used throughout the rest of the chapter and in Excel's commands and options. Details about creating and modifying charts follow. You'll find Excel's charting capabilities give you a lot of control in how you can present data.

Overview of Charting

You can make a lot of choices regarding the appearance of a chart in Excel, but the basic process for creating charts is the same. You begin with Excel's default (or automatic) chart, then modify it to your liking.

The process is easy. First, select the worksheet data that you want to chart, including any column and row headings that might apply. Select the File-Open command and choose the Chart option. This opens a chart window with a column chart that reflects the data you selected in the first step. You can change to a different chart type using the Gallery options. Next, you can modify various elements of the chart, including the axes, titles, patterns, colors, legend and so on. Add descriptive text to the chart if you like. When you're finished, save the chart with the File-Save command.

Charting is really as simple as that. Don't let all the charting commands and options make you think otherwise. By the end of this chapter, you'll be able to create any chart and control various aspects of that chart.

158

Parts of a Chart

Take a few moments to look over the parts of a chart as shown in Figures 9-1 and 9-2. Figure 9-1 shows a basic worksheet ready for charting. Figure 9-2 shows a basic column chart (sometimes called a bar chart) with various elements identified. The chart in Figure 9-2 was created from the data in Figure 9-1. An explanation of each of the chart elements follows.

Data series—The bars, pie wedges, lines or other elements that represent plotted values in a chart are called the data series. For example, a chart might show a set of similar bars that reflects a series of values for the same item. The bars in the series would all have the same pattern. In Figure 9-2, there are two different patterns of bars. Each pattern represents a separate data series. As you can see, data series reflect the individual items being charted. For example, charting the sales for Store 1 versus Store 2 would require two data series—one for each store. Often, data series correspond to rows of data in your worksheet.

Categories—Categories reflect the number of elements in a series. You might have two data series to compare the sales of two different stores, and four categories to compare these sales

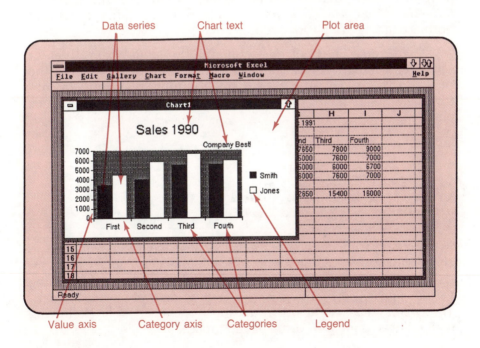

Figure 9-1.   An example worksheet for charting.

Data series   Chart text   Plot area

Figure 9-2.   The parts of a chart.

Value axis   Category axis   Categories   Legend

159

over four quarters. Some charts have only one category, and others have several. Categories are often explained by the category labels below the axis. Categories normally correspond to the number of columns that you have in your chart data, with the category labels coming from the column headings. See Figure 9-2 for an example.

Chart text—Chart text includes all the labels on the chart. Most chart text has to be added to the basic chart. You can control the appearance of labels by changing the type fonts and type styles. You can add text to any part of a chart for explanatory purposes.

Value axis—The value axis is the vertical axis. It reflects the values of the bars, lines or plot points. Excel automatically assigns values to this axis when you create a chart, but you can override the default settings and set the minimum and maximum values. You can also add a label to the value axis that describes what the values represent.

160

Category axis—The category axis is the horizontal axis that contains all the data series and categories in the chart. If you have more than one category, this axis often contains labels that define what each category represents.

Plot area—The plot area contains the actual bars, lines or other representations of the data series. Everything outside the plot area helps explain what's inside the plot area. You can control the appearance of the plot area independently of other chart elements.

Creating a Basic Chart

All charts start out basically the same. You have to create a basic chart with Excel's automatic settings before you can create more customized charts. If desired, you can modify the basic chart using various tools. The first task is to select the data you want to chart. The second task is to bring up the basic chart. The following Quick Steps guide you through the process.

Selecting the Data and Creating the Chart

1. Highlight the data that you want to chart. This can be several rows and columns if desired. Keep in mind that the rows usually reflect the data series and the columns reflect the categories. Be sure to include any row or column titles that apply.

   Selects the highlighted area. Figure 9-3 shows an example. See *A Word About Chart Orientation* later in this chapter for details about the row/column order of a chart.

2. Select the File-New command.

   Brings up a dialog box with three choices.

3. Press Alt-C to select the Chart option, then press Enter to open the new chart window.

   The chart appears with Excel's default options set. Figure 9-4 shows the basic chart.

161

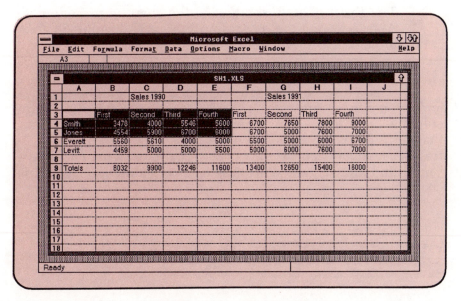

Figure 9-3.   Highlighting the chart data.

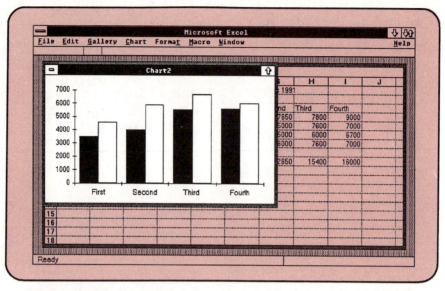

Figure 9-4. The basic chart.

162

> ▶ **Tip:** Excel offers a shortcut to the charting procedure. After selecting the data, simply press F11 or Alt-F1 to create the chart.

In Figures 9-3 and 9-4, the rows translated into data series and the columns into categories. That's because there are more columns than rows. In some instances, you might create a chart that turns your columns into data series and rows into categories. This would occur when you have more rows than columns. You'll find more about controlling chart orientation later in this chapter.

Changing a Chart's Values

A chart and the worksheet that created it are linked. You can make changes in the worksheet and the changes will be reflected in the chart. The chart and the worksheet must both be open for the changes to be immediate. For example, suppose we return to the worksheet from Figure 9-3 and increase one of the values. To return to the worksheet, we press Ctrl-F6 to shift windows, as shown in Figure 9-5. After making a change to the worksheet, we don't have to do anything . . . Excel has already updated the chart window. We can simply press Ctrl-F6 again to view the updated chart, as shown in Figure 9-6.

	A	B	C	D	E	F	G	H	I	J
1			Sales 1990				Sales 1991			
2										
3		First	Second	Third	Fourth	First	Second	Third	Fourth	
4	Smith	3478	4000	7000	5600	6700	7650	7800	9000	
5	Jones	4554	5900	6700	6000	6700	5000	7600	7000	
6	Everett	5560	5610	4000	5000	5500	5000	6000	6700	
7	Levitt	4459	5000	5000	5500	5000	6000	7600	7000	
8										
9	Totals	8032	9900	13700	11600	13400	12650	15400	16000	
10										
11										
12										
13										
14										
15										
16										
17										
18										

Figure 9-5.   *Updating a worksheet.*

163

The automatic update feature is always active, but the chart and its worksheet must be open at the same time. The next section explains how it's possible to open either the chart or worksheet by itself.

Opening, Saving and Closing Charts

Before getting into various chart modifications, let's look at how to open, close and save charts. Since you've already seen how to open, close and save worksheets, this procedure will not seem like anything new. To save a chart, simply make sure that the chart

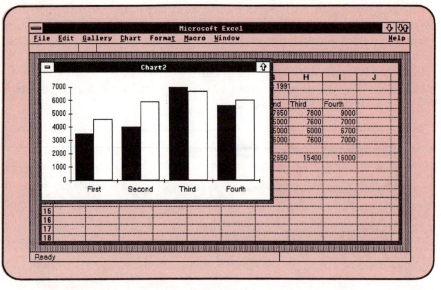

Figure 9-6. *The chart reflects the worksheet modification.*

window is in view, then use the File-Save or File-Save As command just as you would save a worksheet. You'll be asked to name the chart and specify the DOS path to which it should be saved. You can close the chart window using the File-Close command.

Note that charts are not saved with the worksheets that created them. Rather, they become separate and independent files on disk. Excel automatically applies the file extension *.XLC* when you save a chart. You can, of course, add your own extension if desired. You can open a chart without opening the worksheet that created it. And you can open a worksheet without its charts. If you change the values in the worksheet when the chart is not open, the chart will not be updated automatically to reflect those changes. Worksheets and charts are separate files, although they are linked together. Excel knows which worksheets created which charts.

To open an existing chart, use the File-Open command just as you would on a worksheet, as discussed in Chapter 3. If you enter the name of the chart to open it, be sure to include the file extension (.XLC) along with the file name. If the worksheet that created the chart is already open, Excel will automatically update the chart to reflect any changes you've made to the worksheet. If the worksheet is not open, Excel gives you the choice of updating the chart with the most current data from the worksheet, or leaving the chart as is. This message is shown in Figure 9-7.

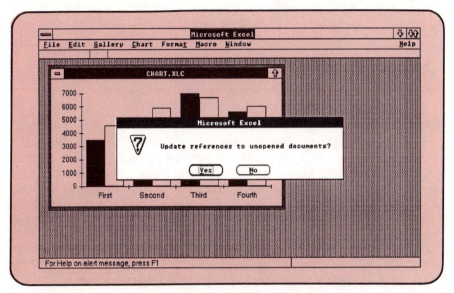

Figure 9-7.   If you open a chart without the worksheet, Excel offers to update the chart.

165

If you choose to update the chart, Excel finds the worksheet and changes the chart to reflect any worksheet modifications. However, the worksheet will not be opened. If you choose not to update the chart, Excel will leave the current values alone. Following is a summary of these rules:

▶ After a chart is created from a worksheet, you can save it using the File-Save command.

▶ When a worksheet and its chart are open at the same time, changes made to the worksheet are immediately reflected in the chart.

▶ If a chart is not open, changes made to its worksheet are not reflected by the chart.

▶ If you open a chart without first opening the worksheet, Excel offers to update the chart with the latest version of the worksheet. This option is useful if the worksheet has been changed without the chart.

As mentioned earlier, Excel remembers which worksheets created which charts. However, if you change the name of a worksheet, delete it or move it to a different subdirectory, Excel may ask that you locate the worksheet so it can re-establish the relationship between the chart and the worksheet.

A Word About Chart Orientation

166

There may be times when Excel produces a chart from a high-lighted range, and the chart is "backward." The data series appears where categories should be, and vice versa. Consider the example in Figure 9-8. This chart uses the same data as the chart in Figure 9-6, but the orientation has been changed. Rather than showing the salespeople as the data series and the quarters as categories, this chart shows the quarters as data series and the salespeople as categories.

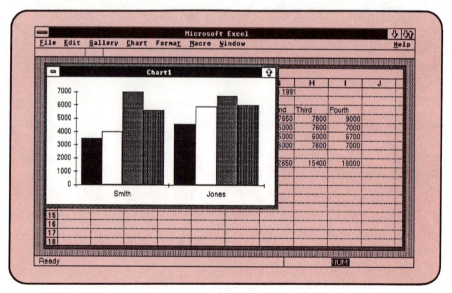

Figure 9-8.   Changing the orientation of the chart in Figure 9-6.

If the orientation can be different like this, how does Excel know which orientation to use? Well, Excel makes a guess, based on your selected data. If you have more columns than rows, then the columns become the categories. If you have more rows than columns, then the rows become categories.

You can always change Excel's orientation for a chart if Excel's guess is wrong. Following are the Quick Steps.

Q **Changing a Chart's Orientation**

1. Close the incorrect chart to remove it from view.

   This should return you to the worksheet.

2. Highlight the chart data, then select the Edit-Copy command.

3. Open a new chart by selecting the command File-New, choosing the Chart option and pressing Enter.

   Brings up a blank chart window. The chart is blank because nothing is highlighted in the worksheet.

167

4. Select the Edit-Paste Special command.

   The dialog box shown in Figure 9-9 appears.

5. Change the Values In option from Rows to Columns or from Columns to Rows, depending on its current setting. Then press Enter. Simply change the setting to the opposite option.

   The chart appears in the window with its new orientation.

Changing a Chart's Size and Shape

Excel creates all new charts at a standard size and shape. This is another of the many defaults that Excel uses when creating new charts. You can change the proportions of the chart. This process is as simple as changing the chart window.

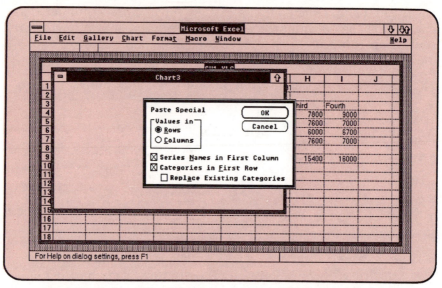

Figure 9-9. *The Edit-Paste Special dialog box.*

168

Press the Alt key then the - (hyphen) key to invoke the Control menu for the chart. From this menu, choose the Size option. You can now change the size of the chart window by using the commands discussed in Chapter 4. By changing the window proportions, you effectively change the proportions of the chart. Figures 9-10 and 9-11 show the sample chart with two different window proportions.

After changing the chart window, be sure to save the changes with the File-Save command. Later, when you print this chart, you can choose to keep the proportions you see on the screen or you can override them. *Printing a Chart* later in this chapter explains the details.

Changing the Chart Type

Excel offers several types of charts for your data. You'll find that certain chart types are best for certain situations. Following is information about how to change the chart type and an overview of the chart types offered by Excel.

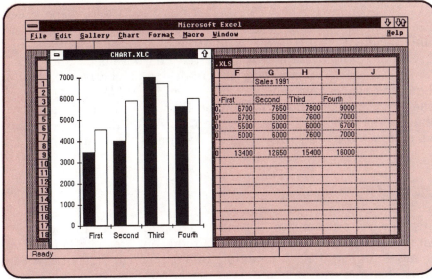

Figure 9-10. *Making a chart taller than normal.*

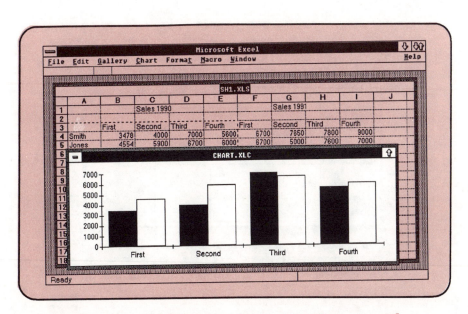

Figure 9-11. *Making a chart wider than normal.*

You can switch between the various chart types at any time. Simply display the basic chart on screen so that the chart window is active. Then, select the desired chart type from the Gallery menu. For example, to get a pie chart, select Gallery-Pie. This will bring up a palette of pre-designed charts within the type you requested. Each variation is numbered. Choose one of the variations by typing its number, then press Enter. The active chart will change to reflect your choice. Following is a list of the chart types offered in the Gallery menu and their variations.

Area Charts

170

Area charts are similar to stacked column charts in that they show how items combine to form a total. But area charts provide a more dramatic representation of the change in values over time. The top of the area chart reflects the total of all elements beneath it. Figure 9-12 shows the Gallery-Area formats, and Figure 9-13 shows an example of format 1.

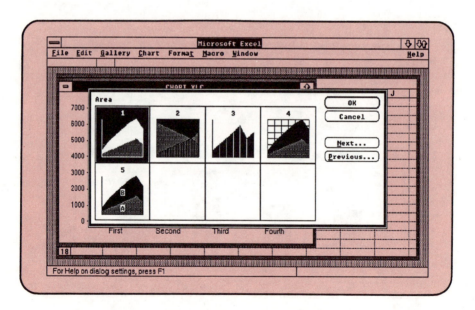

Figure 9-12.   The Gallery-Area options.

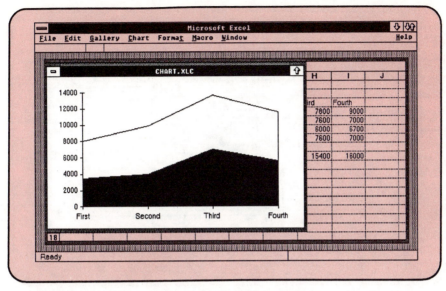

Figure 9-13.   An example area chart.

171

To create an area chart, simply begin with the default chart provided by Excel, then select the desired format from the Gallery-Area command.

Bar Charts

Bar charts are horizontal representation of column charts and are often called histograms. Bar charts emphasize the performance of a group of items. Often, different patterns are not required for bar chart data series. Figure 9-14 shows the Gallery-Bar formats, and Figure 9-15 shows an example of format 1.

Column Charts

Column charts show the relationships between items over a period of time. The columns make it easy to compare the values of items in each category. You can also get an idea of how an item has changed its value over the course of the categories, but area and line charts are best for viewing value trends. Column charts are best for comparing two or more items. Figure 9-16 shows the various column charts available in the Gallery-Column option. Figure 9-17 is an example of chart 1.

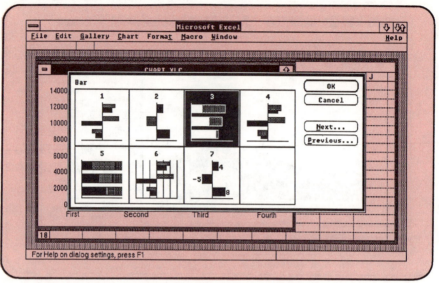

Figure 9-14.   The Gallery-Bar options.

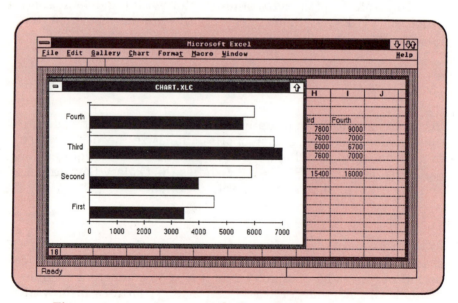

Figure 9-15.   An example bar chart.

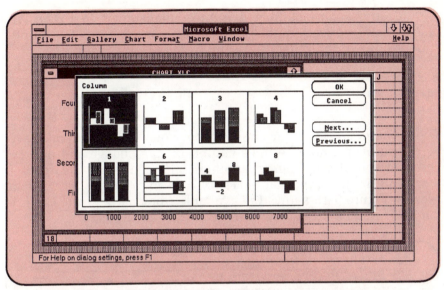

Figure 9-16.   The Gallery-Column options.

173

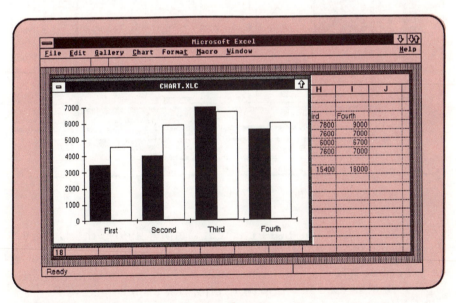

Figure 9-17.   A column chart.

Column chart number 1 is the default chart in Excel. All new charts appear in this format. To change formats, simply choose one of the others from the Gallery-Column options.

Line Charts

Line charts are ideal for showing how one or more items have changed over time. The lines emphasize the change and not the comparison of one item to another. Line charts are also useful for plotting numerous categories of data for a few different data series. Figure 9-18 shows the available line charts in the Gallery menu. Figure 9-19 shows chart type 2 from this list.

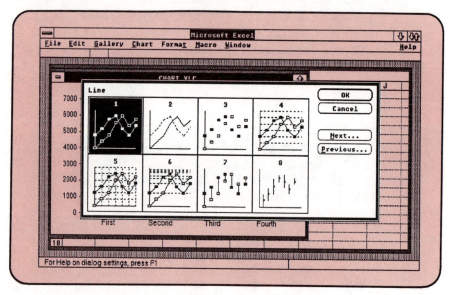

Figure 9-18.   The Gallery-Line options.

After a chart has been created, simply choose the Gallery-Line command and select the desired chart format.

Format 7 is a special type of line chart, called a *hilo* chart. This format is used to show two values for each category. To create a hilo chart, select two rows of data (and as many columns as you like). The first row will represent the high value and the second will represent the low value. Since this is a category-oriented chart, the data series have little bearing on the data.

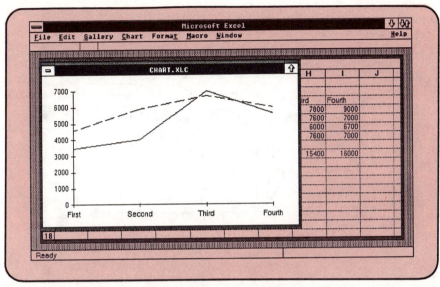

Figure 9-19.   An example line chart.

175

Format 8 is called a *hilo-close* chart. It is similar to the hilo chart, but uses three values for each category: a high, a low and a closing value. Hilo-close charts are often used for stock market analysis. Be sure to select exactly three rows of data. The first row is the high, the second is the low and the third is the closing value.

Pie Charts

Pie charts are the ideal way to show how each data series compares to the total. Pie charts can plot only one category of data, but each wedge of the pie represents a different data series. If you need to show more than one category, consider using a stacked column or area chart instead. Figure 9-20 shows the Gallery-Pie options, and Figure 9-21 shows pie type 3.

First create a chart, which will appear as a column chart with only one category of data. Then, choose the Gallery-Pie command and select the desired format. If you selected more than one category, the pie chart will use only the first.

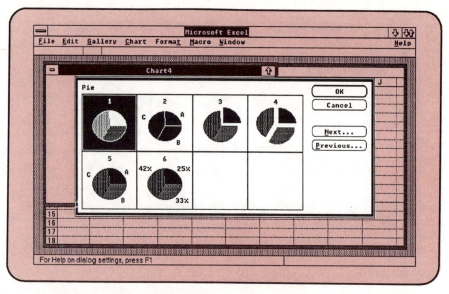

176

Figure 9-20.   The Gallery-Pie options.

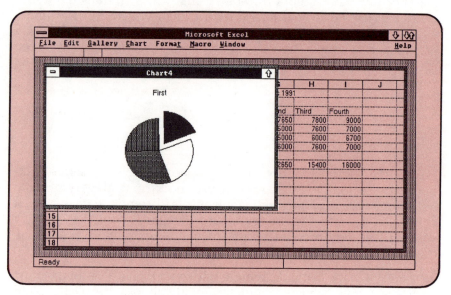

Figure 9-21.   An example pie chart.

Scatter Charts

Scatter charts are used to plot values on x and y axes. On a scatter chart, the category axis does not exist. Instead you have two value axes: one horizontal and one vertical. Excel plots the points on the x and y axes.

Creating a scatter chart requires a slightly different procedure than other charts. First, you should highlight two columns of information. These two columns represent the two values for each plot point. In other words, the values in both columns will be used to plot each point. The first column represents the horizontal value, and the second column is the vertical value. The number of rows determines the number of points. Figure 9-22 shows an example.

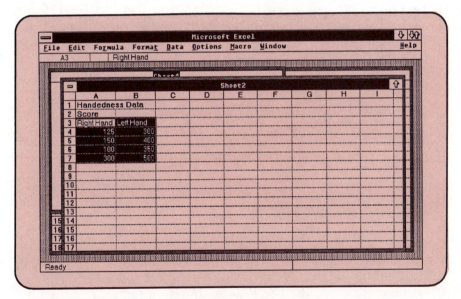

Figure 9-22.   Highlight two columns for a scatter chart.

Next, enter the Edit-Copy command to copy the data. Choose the File-New command and select the Chart option to open a new chart. The chart window should be empty. Now select the Edit-Paste Special command and press Alt-F to select the Categories in First Column option. If the first row of the selected data contains labels (as in the example), then press Alt-N to select the Series Names in First Row option. Press Enter when finished.

The final step is to select one of the scatter chart formats from the Gallery-Scatter menu. Figure 9-23 shows the available formats, and Figure 9-24 shows an example of format 1.

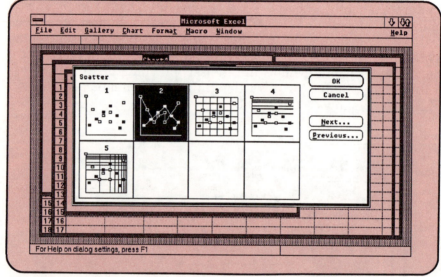

Figure 9-23. *The Gallery-Scatter formats.*

Combination Charts

Combination charts display information using two different types of charts. Like all charts, combination charts begin as the default column chart. Then, when you select one of the combination formats from the Gallery-Combination menu, Excel splits the data series into two groups: a *main chart* group and an *overlay chart* group. Each group will get half of the data series in the chart. The main chart group gets the first half and the overlay group gets the second half. If there is an odd number of data series, then Excel places the extra series in the main chart group.

The main chart group is formatted with one chart type and the overlay group is formatted with a different type. Figure 9-25 shows the Gallery-Combination formats, and Figure 9-26 shows an example of format 4.

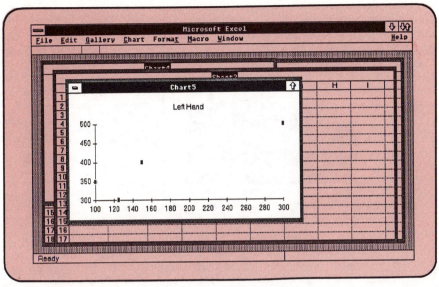

Figure 9-24.   Example scatter chart.

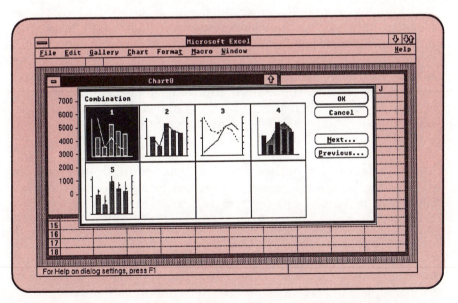

Figure 9-25.   The Gallery-Combination options.

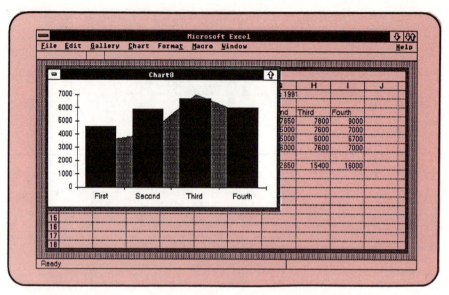

180

Figure 9-26.   An example combination chart.

Remember that Excel splits the data series in half (or as close to half as possible). However, you might want to control how many series get into each group. For example, you might want only one data series in the overlay chart group and all the rest in the main group. You can control this split, and here's how. After creating the combination chart, select the command Format-Overlay. Then press Alt-F to change the First Series in Overlay Chart option. Enter the number of the series with which the overlay chart should begin. The overlay chart will contain this data series and all series after this one. For example, if you have six data series in the chart and you want only the last two in the overlay group, enter a 5 as the First Series in Overlay Chart value. This places series 5 and 6 in the overlay group.

Note that changes to the overlay chart are limited to those options found in the Format-Overlay command. However, the main chart portion of the combination chart is affected by all charting commands—just like any other chart type. The rest of this chapter discusses some of these commands. Remember, these commands affect only the main chart when used with combination charts.

Changing Axis Labels and Scales

Excel automatically scales the value axis for your charts to best fit the minimum and maximum values being charted. However, you might need to customize the values along the vertical axis. You can set the minimum and maximum values, as well as the number of intermediate points along the axis. These intermediate points are called *major units* and *minor units*. You can set the vertical axis scale using the following Quick Steps.

Q **Setting the Vertical Axis Scale**

1. With the chart window active, press the ↑ key until the vertical axis is highlighted.

   Figure 9-27 shows what the vertical axis looks like when it's highlighted. Notice the boxes at each end. Each time you press ↑ a different chart element is highlighted.

2. Select the Format-Scale command.

   The dialog box shown in Figure 9-28 appears. This box contains various options for changing the vertical axis. Each option is discussed following these steps.

3. Enter values for the desired options and press Enter when finished.

   The chart will change to reflect the values you set. ☐

181

 To select the vertical axis, simply click the mouse on the axis line. The boxes will appear at each end of the line.

Following is a description of each option in the Format-Axis dialog box (for vertical axes):

Minimum specifies the low value on the axis. Values less than this minimum will not be visible on the chart.

Maximum specifies the high value on the axis. Values above this maximum will be out of view above the chart.

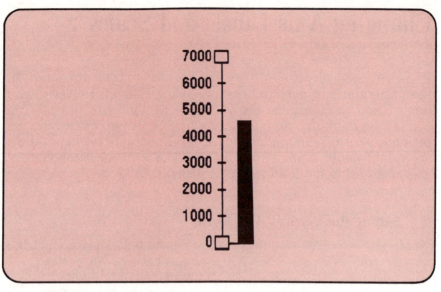

182

Figure 9-27.   Selecting the vertical axis.

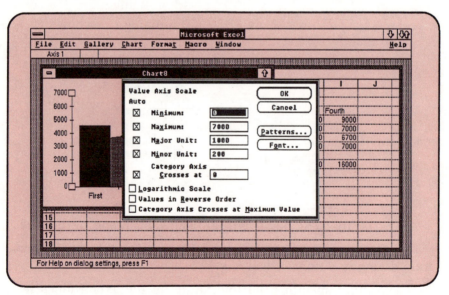

Figure 9-28.   The Format-Scale options.

Major Unit specifies the number of divisions between the high and low values. Each division will be labeled numerically. Enter a number by which the maximum value divides evenly.

Minor Unit specifies the number of tick marks between the major units. Enter a number by which the major unit value divides evenly, or enter the same value as the Major Unit to display no tick marks. Minor unit tick marks are not labeled as are the major units. They are simply cross-hatch lines on the axis. Also, most charts start out with the minor unit tick marks set to invisible. You can make them visible using the formatting options discussed next.

Crosses at specifies the horizontal position of the vertical axis. That is, the position along the category axis where the vertical axis appears. When using this feature on Bar charts, the category and value axes are reversed.

Logarithmic Scale changes the axis to a logarithmic scale.

183

Values in reverse order charts the values in reverse order (that is, with the highest value at the bottom and lowest at the top). This option can be useful for organizing combination charts.

Category Axis Crosses at Maximum Value makes the value axis cross the category axis at the last (maximum) value on the chart. This option appears for scatter charts only. It makes the value axis cross the category axis at the last (maximum) value on the chart.

Formatting the Vertical Axis

Besides controlling the axis values and positioning the tick marks along the axis, you can also choose from a number of tick mark formats. After setting the values, choose the Format-Patterns command (make sure that the vertical axis is still highlighted when you select this command). The dialog box shown in Figure 9-29 appears.

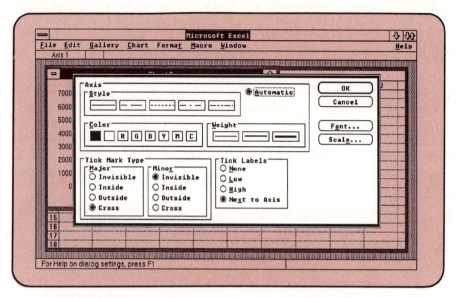

Figure 9-29. The Format-patterns dialog box.

184

Notice that there are three major groups of options. The Axis options include the style, color and weight of the axis line. The Tick Mark Type options include styles for the major and minor tick marks. The Tick Labels options control the appearance of the scale numbers that appear along the value axis.

Select the desired group of options by pressing the Alt key with the letter of the option group. Then use the arrow keys to highlight the desired option within that group. Choosing the Automatic option lets Excel control the appearance of the axis line. Note that the minor tick marks are normally in the Invisible position. This means that your Minor Unit changes in the Format-Scale command will not be visible. You can make the minor tick marks visible by choosing one of the other Minor options. Experiment with these settings for best results. Figure 9-30 shows a few different combinations.

Changing the Patterns of Data Series

Many people like to change the colors and/or patterns of the data series for special effects. While Excel's default patterns and colors

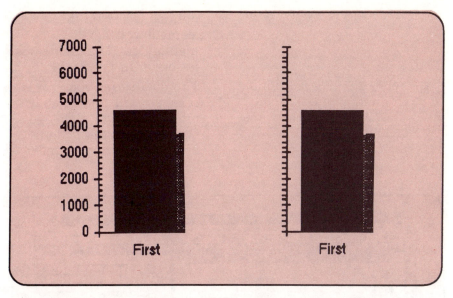

Figure 9-30. *Some tick mark formatting examples.*

serve the purpose of distinguishing one data series from another, you might find some patterns and colors more attractive than others. For example, you might want to remove all patterns and use only color. Changing the pattern of a data series is done with the Format-Patterns command. You can choose from a number of patterns, including those already used by other data series in the same chart. The following Quick Steps give the details.

Q Changing the Data Series Patterns

1. With the chart window active, press the ↑ key until the desired data series is highlighted.

    A highlighted data series contains small white squares in each of the bars, pie wedges or other plot elements as shown in Figure 9-31.

2. Select the Format-Patterns command.

    The Format-Patterns dialog box appears. This dialog box is slightly different from the Format Patterns box you used with the Axis. Excel changes the options based on the element you have highlighted. The dialog box is shown in Figure 9-32.

3. Select the desired options in the dialog box, then press Enter to accept the changes or Esc to reject them.

The data series you selected will immediately reflect the pattern changes. Details about the pattern options are provided next. □

186

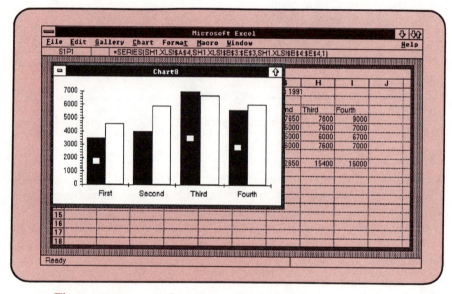

Figure 9-31.   Selecting a data series.

To select a data series with the mouse, simply click on the desired series, such as one of the bars in a bar chart.

The Format-Patterns options are divided into two groups for the data series. The Border options affect the perimeter of the highlighted element, including the style, thickness and color of the border line. The Area options control the inside of the element, such as its pattern and color. Most of these options are self explanatory. Just press the Alt key with the letter of the desired option group (or use the Tab key). Then press the arrow keys to choose an option within that group.

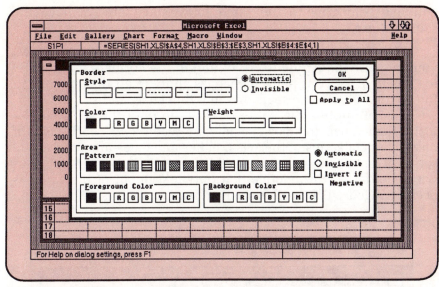

Figure 9-32. **The Format-Patterns dialog box for data series.**

187

If you have a color system, keep in mind that the patterns have two parts: the foreground and the background. Each part can be a different color. The foreground is the pattern itself and the background is the color on which the pattern is drawn. Experiment with the foreground and background colors to see how these work. Note that the solid pattern (the first pattern in the list) provides the solid version of whichever foreground color you choose.

> **Tip:** You can remove all patterns from the graph and use only colors for the data series by selecting the solid pattern for each data series.

As usual, the Automatic option tells Excel to take care of choosing the colors and patterns. The Invisible and Apply to All options are most useful when your chart contains only one data series. When a chart has only one data series, you are able to change each element within the series independently. For example, on a column chart containing only one data series, Excel lets you change the pattern of each column independently of the others even though they belong to the same series. Normally, columns belonging to the same series must always have the same pattern.

Therefore, when your chart contains only one data series, you must use the Apply to All option in the Format-Patterns dialog box to make your pattern changes apply to all the columns in the column chart, line segments in a line chart and so on. Otherwise, Excel applies the pattern change to only the selected element. Remember, this is a special case when your charts contain only one data series. Otherwise, pattern changes affect an entire series at once. As an example, Figure 9-33 shows a line chart with one data series. Notice that only a segment of the line has been changed with the Format-Patterns command.

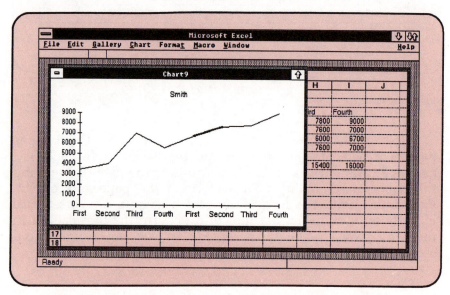

Figure 9-33.   Changing a portion of a data series.

Changing the Category Labels

If you're not satisfied with the category labels that go with your chart, you can change them. Any text or value can be used as a category label. Following are the Quick Steps.

Changing the Category Labels

1. If the desired category labels are not already part of the worksheet, enter them into any worksheet range. Use the same number of labels as there are categories in the chart. Figure 9-34 shows an example.

2. Select the range containing the desired labels, then use the Edit-Copy command to copy this data.

   Excel places the marquee around the labels.

3. Activate the chart window. Assuming the chart is open, you can use Ctrl-F6 or the Window menu to do this.

   The chart, with its old category labels should now be in view.

   189

4. Select the Edit-Paste Special command.

   The Paste Special dialog box appears.

5. Make sure that the Categories in First Row and the Replace Existing Categories options are checked. If your new category labels were in a column rather than a row, the Categories in First Row option will read Categories in First Column. Use Alt-F and Alt-A to check or uncheck them. Press Enter when finished.

   The category labels change, as shown in the example in Figure 9-35.

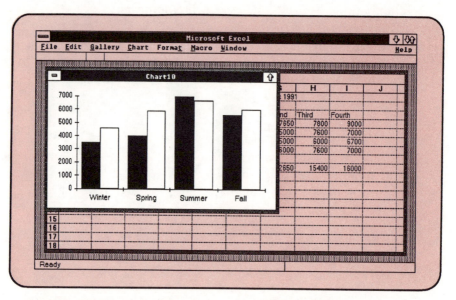

Figure 9-34.   Adding new category labels to the worksheet.

Figure 9-35.   Pasting the new category labels into an existing chart using Edit-Paste Special.

Adding Chart Elements

Now let's take a look at some of the special elements you can add to your charts to enhance readability. The steps for adding and formatting these elements are described in the next sections.

Adding Labels

You can add all kinds of titles, subtitles and labels to your chart. Highlight a chart element and select the Chart-Attach Text command. Following are the Quick Steps for this procedure.

Q Attaching Text to a Chart

191

1. Highlight the desired chart element using the ↑ and → keys. The ↑ key highlights a different element each time you press it. When there are more than one of a particular type of element (for example, there are two axes), use the → key to move among them. Using the mouse, simply click on the desired element to highlight it.

2. Select the Chart-Attach Text command. Make any required changes, then press Enter.

   The Attach Text dialog box appears. It shows which element you have highlighted. Use this box to confirm or modify your selection. When you press Enter, Excel adds a text box to the chart. This box will contain temporary text as a place holder.

3. Type your new text. Press Enter when finished.

   The new text replaces the temporary text. □

The advantage to attaching text using the Attach Text command is that Excel adjusts the chart to make room for the added text. However, you are not limited to adding text to the chart elements listed in the Attach Text dialog box. In fact, you don't have to attach text to any particular element at all. To add descriptive text, first make sure that no chart element is highlighted. If a chart element is already highlighted, use the following Quick Steps to unhighlight.

Q Unhighlighting Chart Elements With the Keyboard

1. Select the Chart-Add Arrow command.

   Places an arrow on the chart.

2. Select the Chart-Delete Arrow command.

   Removes the arrow you just added and leaves the chart elements unhighlighted. ☐

192

To unhighlight all chart elements with the mouse, click the mouse just inside the edge of the chart window, as close to the edge as possible.

After unhighlighting the chart element, begin typing your text and press Enter when finished. After pressing Enter, the text will appear on the chart. Figure 9-36 shows an example.

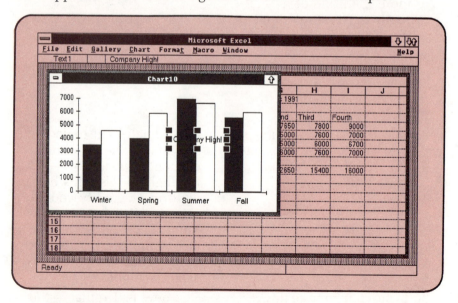

Figure 9-36.   Adding descriptive text to a chart.

The next step is to move the text to the desired position on the chart. Using the keyboard, first make sure that the text box is highlighted as shown in Figure 9-36. Now select the Format-Move command. The text box becomes a special moveable box. Use the four arrow keys to move the text to a new location. Press Enter when finished. If you have a mouse, simply click on the new text and drag it to the desired location. Figure 9-37 shows an example of moving text.

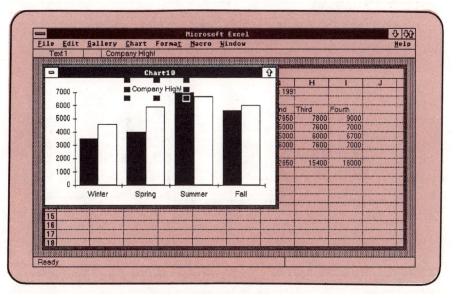

Figure 9-37.   *Moving a text box.*

193

To remove any added text from the chart, simply highlight the text using the ↑ key, then press the Backspace key and enter. The text will be removed.

> ▶ **Tip:** In the previous discussion, you learned how to add and remove an arrow in order to unhighlight the chart elements. Just select the Chart-Add Arrow command. This places the arrow on the chart. You can now move the arrow with the Format-Move command as described for moving a text box. Using the Format-Size command, you can change the size and direction of the arrow.

Adding A Legend

Adding a chart legend is easy. Excel already knows which chart labels make up the legend—the data series labels in the first column of the chart range. To display these labels in a legend, simply use the Chart-Add Legend command. The chart adjusts to make room for the legend as shown in Figure 9-38.

194

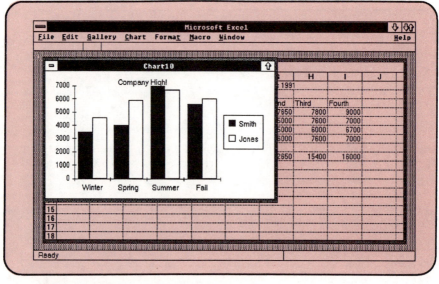

Figure 9-38.   Adding a legend.

You can change the placement of the legend by selecting the Format-Legend command when the legend box is highlighted. (As usual, use ↑ key or the mouse to highlight the legend.) The Format-Legend dialog box offers four positions for the legend box: Bottom, Corner, Top and Vertical. Experiment for best results. You might also try changing the proportions of the chart to accommodate the legend box.

Adding Gridlines

Another element you can add to a chart is a grid. A grid appears in the plot area of the chart and is useful for emphasizing the vertical scale of the data series. To add gridlines, select the

Chart-Gridlines command. Excel presents the four Gridline options. You can add major and minor gridlines for the vertical (value) axis and/or horizontal (category) axis. After adding the gridlines, you can change their colors and patterns as described in the next section.

Changing the Fonts and Patterns of Chart Elements

You can change the font of any text showing on the chart. This includes attached text, descriptive text, axis titles and legend entries. Simply highlight the desired element and select the Format-Font command. Excel's list of fonts appears on the screen. Select the desired font, size, style and color from the list and press Enter when finished. It is wise to select a printer font rather than a screen font, because using a screen font may cause the printer to run out of memory while you're trying to print.

195

You can also change the patterns of many elements. This includes text boxes and interiors, legend boxes and interiors, axis lines, arrows, gridlines, the chart background, the plot area and data series. As you have probably guessed, first highlight the desired element, then use the Format-Patterns command. Select from pattern options provided, then press Enter.

What You've Learned

In this chapter you've learned just about everything relating to Excel's charting capabilities. You discovered how to select chart data, create a basic chart and then modify the chart. These modifications include changing the chart type, adding special elements and changing the chart's orientation. Following are some of the points covered in this chapter.

▶ Charts consist of various parts or elements. These elements can be highlighted by pressing the ↑ and → keys. Often, you must highlight an element before applying a particular command.

▶ To begin a basic chart, highlight the chart data on the worksheet, including row and column labels if applicable. Then use the File-New command to open a new chart window.

▶ When the chart window and the worksheet window are open at the same time, changes made to the worksheet are immediately reflected in the chart.

▶ If you make changes to the worksheet when the chart is not open, Excel will update the chart the next time it is opened when the worksheet is open.

▶ If you open a chart without the worksheet open, Excel will ask if you want to update the chart to reflect the most current changes to the worksheet. Excel asks this even if you have not made changes to the worksheet.

196 ▶ You can change the row/column orientation of a chart by using the Edit-Paste Special command.

▶ Changing the size and shape of the chart window changes the size and shape of the chart itself.

▶ Use the Gallery options to change the chart type.

▶ Use the Format-Patterns dialog box to change the pattern of almost any chart element, including the border and interior of the element.

▶ Use the Format-Font command to change the font of any chart text.

▶ Add legends with the Chart-Add Legend command.

▶ Add chart titles using the Chart-Attach Text command.

Chapter 10

Managing Data with Excel

In This Chapter

- ▶ *The structure of a database*
- ▶ *Starting and activating a database in Excel*
- ▶ *Inserting records*
- ▶ *Viewing records*
- ▶ *Editing and deleting records*
- ▶ *Sorting data*

This chapter explains how to use Excel to store data as a database. The database feature lets you expand on the standard commands and options offered for worksheet data, giving you special commands and options that apply directly to database data. The only difference between database data and worksheet data is that database data has been "activated" as a database. In this chapter you'll discover reasons for using databases in Excel and the basics for setting them up, adding to them and sorting them.

Database Structure

Using Excel for database operations is really just an extension of
the worksheet features. The only difference is in the way you have
to access the data. When you have multiple records—such as a list
of similar items—and when you have to search those records for
particular groups, then you probably need to set up the information as a database. Some examples include customer back orders,
sales records, book lists and address lists, which are shown in Figures 10-1 through 10-4.

198

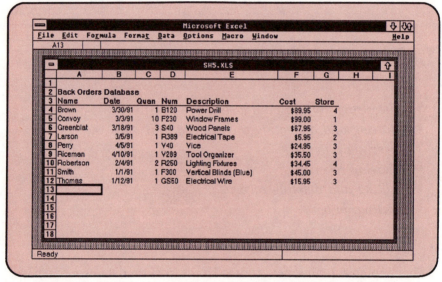

*Figure 10-1.   A sample database of back ordered
merchandise.*

Notice in the examples that the information for each item is
entered across one row. Each row in a database is called a
record. Each record is on a different row, and the pieces of information within the records are spread across the row in different
cells. The cells within a row, which hold the data for the record,
are called *fields*. Notice that each column is labeled with a
unique name that describes what's in that column. The column
headings above each column are called *field names*.

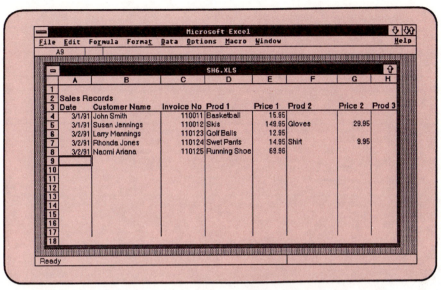

Figure 10-2.   A sample database of sales records.

	Microsoft Excel						

B12

Sheet3

	A	B	C	D	E	F	G
1							
2		Book List					
3		Title	Author	Call No	Subj	Date Pub	
4		Best Known Works	Hawthorn	C.23	Lit	1925	
5		Short Stories	Poe	C.45	Lit	1945	
6		For Whom the Bell Tolls	Hemmingway	C.28	Lit	1969	
7		Lord Jim	Conrad	C.18	Lit	1979	
8		The 17th Earl of Oxford	Ward	D.45	Bio	1929	
9		The Egyptian Gnostics	Doresse	R.12	Rel	1986	
10		First Book of Excel	Van Buren	B.78	Com	1990	
11							

Ready

Figure 10-3.   A sample book list.

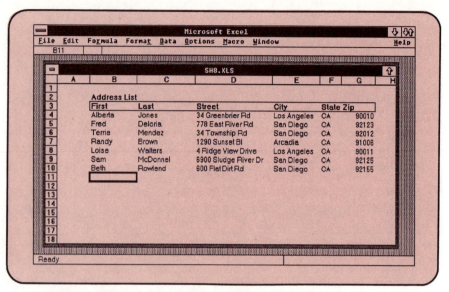

Figure 10-4.   A sample address list.

These are the essential elements of a database in Excel. You'll find that data naturally fits into this pattern and that you hardly have to try to keep database data in the required structure.

Basically, a database is just a group of records entered in a specific way. You might even have been using this structure for your worksheet data all along. The only thing that makes database data different from other worksheet information is that databases contain many similar records that require frequent access and upkeep.

Starting a Database

When you create a database, simply enter the data in the list form described in the previous section. Make sure that each row contains information for a single record and that there are no blank rows (that is, missing records) in the list. Also make sure that you have labeled the columns at the top. The column headings (or field names) must be text labels. There should be no space between the labels and the first record. Use the examples in Figures 10-1 through 10-4 as a guide.

Since the nature of a database is to grow, leave enough room at the bottom of the database for added records. You might, in fact, want to give the database its own area of the worksheet, below everything else, to allow nearly unlimited growth. Another idea is to avoid placing a database to the right or left of other worksheet data. Adding or removing database records can affect adjacent areas of the worksheet. The only absolute requirements are that you must include field names (column headings) for the data and that no blank rows should appear below the field names.

Once the database area and field names are established, you can begin entering data. The easiest way to add information is to use the data form, which is described in the next section. Or, you may just begin typing the information under each column heading. Consider highlighting the database range before entering data. This will cause the pointer to remain in the range as you move from cell to cell with the Tab and Return keys.

201

You do not have to complete each record in the database. In other words, some fields can remain blank. But remember not to leave an entire record blank. You can use formulas to produce some field values. One column, for example, might be calculated from the values in other columns. The PRICE and QUANTITY fields of each record in a Sales Receipt database might be multiplied to produce a TOTAL field for each record. All normal worksheet operations are available for use with your database data.

Activating the Database Features

So far, you have seen how to enter information in a database structure for Excel. But you might be wondering what's so special about this. You might even have been using such a structure for all kinds of data without realizing it. What's special is that you can activate Excel's database features for data that is entered in the correct structure by using the Data-Set Database command.

Highlight all the old or new data you have typed in database format, including all existing records and the column headings at the top. Then select the Data-Set Database command to activate the database.

By activating the database this way, you have added a number of special features that can now be used with the database you selected. The most important feature is the data form, which is useful for inserting new records into the database, deleting records and finding specific records.

> ► **Tip:** You can have more than one database on a worksheet, but only one can be activated at a time. To switch to a different database, simply highlight the area of the worksheet containing the other database and use the Data-Set Database command. Whichever range you've activated last will be the current database.

Adding Records to the Database

Once you activate a database, you can do almost everything with the special data form. For example, you can use the data form to insert new records into the database. You'll find this procedure easier than inserting the records manually at the bottom of the list. And, you can begin using the data form immediately after you create the field names, highlight them and a blank row, and execute the Data-Set Database command. Just use the following Quick Steps.

 Adding New Records with the Data Form

1. Select the Data-Form command.

   Brings the data form into view. The data form displays the fields you have defined in the database structure. Figure 10-5 shows an example.

2. Press Alt-W to start a new record.

   Clears all data from the form so you can enter new information.

3. Type the information for each field in the form. Press Tab to move to the next field or Shift-Tab to move back to a previous field. Press Backspace to correct typing errors. All editing commands are available while you are typing in the data form.

4. When finished with the record, press Alt-W to add another new record or Alt-X to exit the data form and return to the worksheet.

Whether you press Alt-W or Alt-X, the new record will be added to the bottom of the database. ☐

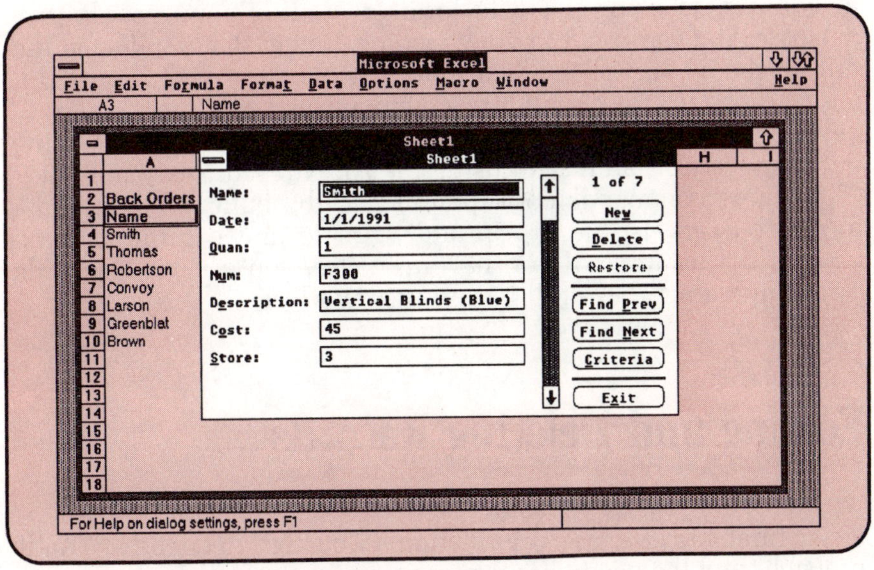

203

Figure 10-5.   The data form.

Data forms are limited to 14 fields. If any of the fields in a database are calculated using formulas, you will be unable to type information for that field in the data form. Instead, Excel assumes that you want to reproduce the formula for all new records and inserts the formula automatically for each new record.

> ▶ **Tip:** After the database is activated, it's best to add records by using the data form. If you type new records into worksheet rows below the existing data, the new records will not be part of the active database. You'll have to reactivate the database to include the new records. However, you can insert new rows into the middle of the database range and enter new records into those rows. This does not require that you reactivate the database. The new records will be part of the active database. Still, the data form provides the easiest way to add new records.

Viewing Database Records

204

In addition to using the data form for adding new records to a database, you can use it to view records. Rather than looking at the full database list, use the data form to view each record individually. Just select the Data-Form command and use the ↑ and ↓ keys to "flip" forward and backward through the database. Using the arrow keys is similar to using the Alt-N (Find Next) and Alt-P (Find Prev) commands corresponding to the buttons on the data form. You can also use PgUp and PgDn to move to the extreme ends of the database. If you have a mouse, you can view records by manipulating the scroll bar on the data form.

Editing and Deleting Records

It's natural for database information to change frequently. You'll probably find the need to return to a previously entered record and change it. Perhaps a customer has moved, and you need to update an address. Or maybe an order has arrived, and you need to mark it as completed. Whatever the reason, updating records is an important part of database management.

You can update records in two ways. First, you can simply move the pointer to the row in which the record appears, then select and update the cells which need changing. Use the editing commands described in Chapter 5.

A second way to edit the information in a record is to use the data form. Simply activate the data form and use the ↓ key to locate the desired record. Press the Tab key to move to the field you want to change. As shown in Figure 10-6, pressing the Tab key highlights the fields.

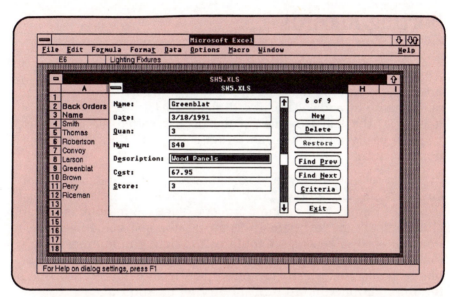

Figure 10-6. **Highlighting a field with the Tab key.**

With the field highlighted, you can simply begin typing new data to completely replace the existing data. Or, if you want to change only a part of the existing data, use the → or ← keys to unhighlight the field. Then use the basic editing commands listed in Chapter 5 to make further changes.

Press Enter or Alt-X to accept your changes, or press Esc to reject them and return to the worksheet.

> ▶ **Tip:** As your database grows larger, using the ↓ key to find records with the data form will get less and less practical. This is when you should turn to the data searching procedures discussed in the next chapter.

Besides editing a record in the database, you can use the data form to delete a record. As with editing, first locate the desired record so it is in view in the data form. Then, press Alt-D to delete the record. Press Enter to accept the deletion and return to the worksheet, or press Alt-R then Enter to restore the deleted record and return to the worksheet.

Sorting Records

Another important aspect of databases is that they usually display information in a sorted (or alphabetical) order. If data is entered randomly into a database, it's difficult to locate information by looking at the list. However, if the data is sorted alphabetically, you can easily look down the sorted column to find the information you want.

206

You rely on this type of sorted order in the "databases" you already use. The phone book, for example, is an alphabetical listing of names and phone numbers. The phone book is sorted alphabetically by last names. As a rule, the last name is the best field for sorting because it contains the data you are most likely to know already. It would do precious little good to sort the phone book numerically by telephone numbers, because that's the information you are probably trying to find out.

The same rule applies to the databases you create in Excel. Sorting is for arranging the data on the piece of information (that is, the field) that you are most likely to already know. You can quickly look over the sorted fields to find the record you want, giving you access to the information in that record that you don't already know. The difference between the Excel database and your phone book is that you can resort the Excel database over and over again using any piece of information in the database. The phone book is stuck with a last name sort. Resorting is particularly useful after you add records to a database.

The final thing to note before sorting your data is that Excel uses one of three different sorting methods for the data, based on the field by which you sort the data. If the field contains text, Excel sorts the records alphabetically. If the field contains numeric data, Excel sorts the records numerically. If the field contains dates, then Excel sorts the records chronologically. Finally, you can sort the data in ascending or descending order: that is, from A to Z or from Z to A. An ascending sort is the most common.

The following Quick Steps show you how to sort data.

Q Sorting the Database

1. Highlight all the records in the database, but do not include the field names at the top.

   Figure 10-7 shows an example.

2. Press the Tab key to position the pointer in the column by which you want the data sorted. For example, if you are sorting by last names, place the pointer in the last name column.

   This prepares the sort command for the *key field*, or the field by which you are sorting the data.

207

3. Select the Data-Sort command.

   The dialog box shown in Figure 10-8 appears, providing choices for the sorting order. Notice that the dialog box contains a reference to the current cell, indicating the column by which you are sorting.

4. Press Enter to sort the data in ascending order. Press Alt-D and then Enter to sort the data in descending order.

   After pressing Enter, the data will be sorted according to the specified key field. Figure 10-9 shows the example database sorted by last names. □

Remember that you can sort and resort the database at any time. When you add records using the data form, they will probably not be entered in alphabetical order, so you might want to resort the database after adding records.

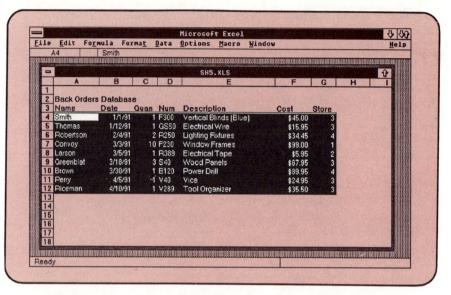

208

Figure 10-7.   Highlighting the database records for sorting.

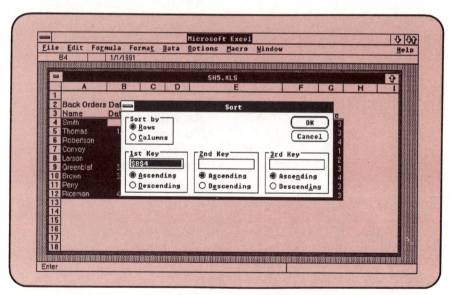

Figure 10-8.   The Data-Sort dialog box.

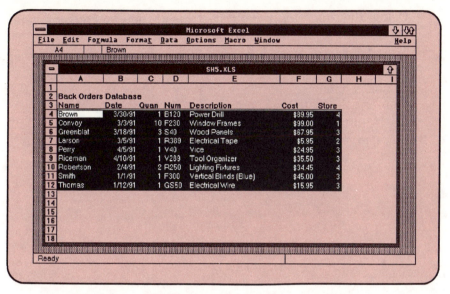

Figure 10-9.   Result of sorting the example database by last names.

What You've Learned

This chapter provided an introduction to Excel's database features. Database data is not much different from any other data you might enter into a worksheet. However, database data usually requires more frequent updating, more complex analyzing and other such management needs. The use of the data form is a key feature in Excel's database capabilities. Following are some points to remember:

▶ Database data consists of records, which are entered in rows of the worksheet. Within each record are fields, which are the cells in each row.

▶ Be sure to include column headings for each column in the database. These are formally known as field names.

▶ There should be no blank records in the database.

▶ Activate a database by highlighting the data and field names and then using the Data-Set Database command. This makes the data form available for future database management needs. You need only do this once.

▶ Using the data form, you can insert new records, delete records and even edit existing records.

▶ The data form also lets you "flip" through the database records one at a time.

▶ To sort a database, highlight the data without the field names, then use the Data-Sort command. The position of the pointer determines the field by which the data is sorted.

▶ You can sort in ascending or descending order.

210

Finding and Extracting Database Records

In This Chapter

▶ *Finding records with the data form*
▶ *Using wild cards and logical operators in search criteria*
▶ *Finding records with a criteria range*
▶ *Deleting batches of records*
▶ *Extracting database records*

This chapter shows you how to find records in a database. To locate records, you must enter criteria into a criteria range or into the data form. This chapter shows you how to enter criteria and the types of criteria you can use. You'll also learn how to delete or extract records from the database.

Finding Records with the Data Form

The easiest way to search for database records is to use the data form. Using the data form, you can locate any record in the database by identifying information in any one of the fields. Finding can be as simple as matching values, such as finding a record that contains "Smith" in the Last Name field. Or you can find records based on more fields, such as all the records with "Smith" in the Last Name field and "NY" in the State field. You can even find records based on special conditions, such as all last names beginning with "S", using wild cards and logical operators.

If more than one record matches the criteria, you can browse through all the matching records. The criteria you select establishes a subset of the database: for example, all records for Smiths in New York.

212

Making a Simple Search

To try a simple search, open a worksheet with database information and activate the database range if it has not already been activated. Then view the data form with the Data-Form command. Figure 11-1 shows an example.

Of course, when it first appears, the data form always shows the first record in the database. Once the data form is in view, you can begin to find records with three easy steps: Press Alt-C to select the Criteria button on the data form; enter the desired criteria into the blank field boxes that are presented; and select the Find Next button by pressing Alt-N. Let's take a look at each of these steps in detail.

The first step is pressing Alt-C to activate the criteria entry form, which is a basically a blank version of the data form. Notice that some of the buttons on the form change when you select the Criteria button. For one thing, the Criteria button changes to the Form button so you can return to the data form whenever you like. Following is a list of the buttons available on the criteria entry form:

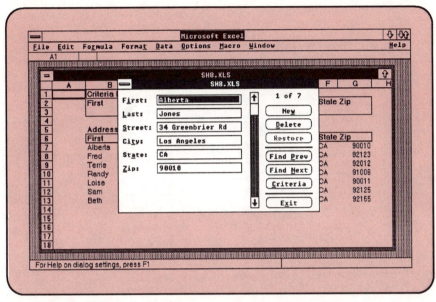

Figure 11-1. **The data form for an address database.**

Clear	If you have entered criteria information into the fields, this button clears that data so you can start over.
Restore	If you have used the Clear button, this button restores the criteria you had on the form.
Find Previous	This button finds the previous record that matches your criteria.
Find Next	This button finds the next record in the database that matches your criteria.
Form	This button returns to the data form without searching for the criteria you've set.
Exit	The Exit button returns you to the worksheet.

The next step is to enter the desired criteria into the fields of the criteria entry form. First use the Tab key to move to that field. Then enter the data that you are trying to match. For example, to find all records for people in San Diego in an address database, enter San Diego into the City field as shown in Figure 11-2.

213

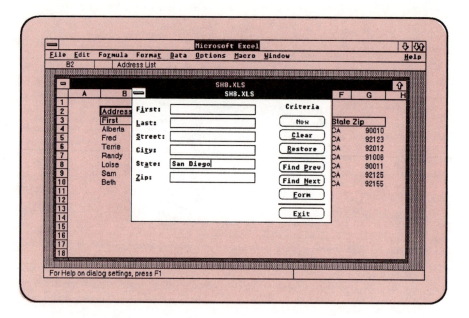

214

Figure 11-2.   Entering criteria for searching.

The last step is to press Alt-N to select the Find Next button. Starting from the first record in the database, the Find Next button locates the *next* record that matches the criteria you selected, such as the criteria shown in Figure 11-3. The Find Next button compares the second and subsequent records with the criteria. Press Alt-N again to find the next matching record and again for the next. You are viewing a subset of the database, skipping all records that do not match the criteria. Of course, using the Find Previous button flips through the records backward. When you reach the last matching record, Excel beeps to indicate that no more exist.

You can view other (non-matching) records in the database by using the ↑ and ↓ keys in the usual way. But the Find Previous and Find Next buttons will show you only the matching records. Pressing Alt-C again takes you back to the criteria form where you can enter new criteria or modify the existing criteria.

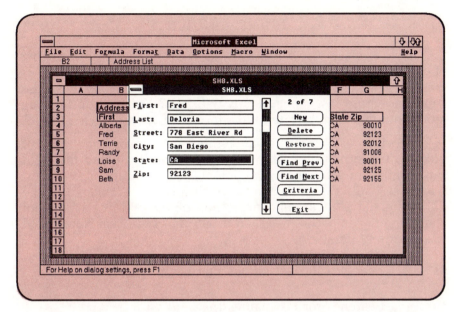

Figure 11-3.   Finding the first matching record.

Let's try specifying more criteria fields in the database shown in Figures 11-2 and 11-3 to narrow the matching records down to only one. We can press Alt-C to return to the criteria screen. Then, with San Diego still entered in the City field, we could enter McDonnel in the Last Name field. Pressing Alt-N would show us the records that match both criteria: people who have the last name of McDonnel and who live in San Diego.

Note that when you begin searching with Alt-N, Excel begins searching from the current record displayed in the data form. If you are currently at the first record in the database, Excel doesn't "look at" the current (first) record but finds the next (second) record in the database that matches. If you are not at the beginning of the database, Excel selects the *next* record that matches rather than the *first* record in the database that matches. For example, let's say you have a database where records 4, 6 and 10 have "Smith" in the Last Name field. If record 6 is the current record and you search for "Smith," record number 10 will be the first record Excel finds. Therefore, it's a good practice to jump to the first record of the database before starting your search.

Making a More Complex Match

So far, you've seen how to locate records using direct matching of criteria. But direct matches can limit your ability to find information. For example, what if you want to find all people in the database whose last name *begins with* a B? You can do it using more complex search criteria—criteria that include a *wild card*.

A wild card is a special symbol that takes the place of unknown information in the search criteria. By using the wild card symbol in different ways, you can get all kinds of powerful searches. The wild card symbol is simply the * (asterisk). The following list shows some examples of the wild card symbol when entered as part of the search criteria in the Last Name field of an address database:

216

M*	Searches for last names that begin with M
***m**	Searches for last names that end with m
m	Searches for last names that contain an m in them, but which do not begin or end with m
M*m	Searches for last names that begin with M and end with m

Simply enter the wild card in one of the ways shown above. You can use the wild card with numeric entries as well as text.

You might need to find records based on special conditions, such as all records that *do not contain* a particular criteria. Using numeric fields, you can find all values *less than* or *greater than* a particular criteria. To accomplish these matches, you must include one of the following logical operators with your criteria:

<>	Does not equal
>	Is greater than
<	Is less than

$>=$ Is greater than or equal to

$<=$ Is less than or equal to

▶ **Note:** With the exception of the $<>$ operator, these logical operators are meant for numeric information and dates. For example, entering ›10000 finds all records with values greater than 10000. But the $>$ operator (as well as $<>=$ and $<=$) has no purpose for fields containing text.

As an example, suppose you want to find everyone in an address database whose first name is not Fred. Your criteria would look like Figure 11-4.

217

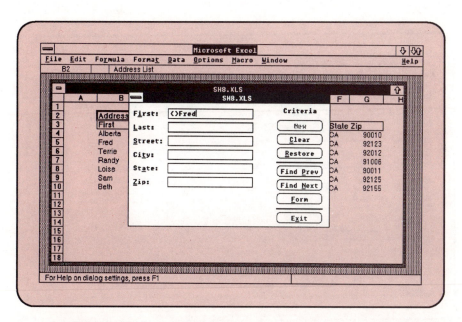

Figure 11-4.   *Entering logical operators in criteria.*

Now the Find Next and Find Previous buttons will ignore all records with Fred in the First Names field. Experimenting with these operators can help you get familiar with their results. Remember that Excel begins searching at the current record being displayed in the data form. To search from the beginning of the database, be sure to move to the first record before entering the criteria.

Using a Criteria Range

So far you've seen how to find records in the database by using the data form to establish search criteria. When searching with the data form, you can flip through all matching records. The more search criteria you include, the fewer records you will have to search through to find the specific data you need.

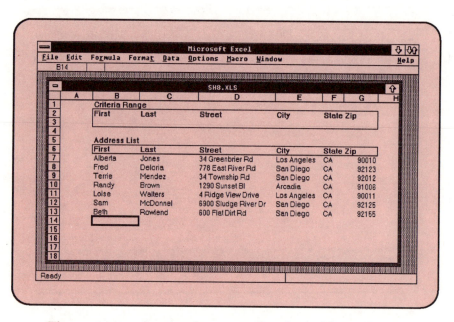

Figure 11-5. A criteria range for the address list.

Another way to search for database records is to use a *criteria range* on the worksheet. A criteria range is a range of cells that contains the field names and criteria entries you want to use. In a way, the procedure is like duplicating the data form on the worksheet. Figure 11-5 shows a typical criteria range.

Notice that the criteria range includes all the field names plus a blank row beneath these names. You simply enter the criteria into the blank row just as you would enter it into the data form. You may be wondering why you would use a criteria range when you can use the data form in much the same way. Here are the advantages to using a criteria range:

▶ You can delete a batch of records at once using criteria entered into the criteria range. Using the data form, you can delete only one record at a time.

▶ You can extract records from the database and place them in a worksheet range. The extracted data matches the criteria in the criteria range. You cannot extract records using the data form.

219

▶ You can establish more complex criteria than available with the data form. Besides matching data with direct entries, wildcards and logical operators, you can also use OR logic in the criteria range. For example, you can find all people in your database whose first name is Fred OR Sam. The data form allows AND conditions only.

The only disadvantage to using a criteria range is that it's not as simple as the data form. But you might trade some of the data form's simplicity for the additional features offered by the criteria range. The following Quick Steps show how to create a criteria range. Then you will learn how to use this range for finding, deleting and extracting records.

Q Creating a Criteria Range

1. Type or copy the database field names into a row anywhere on the worksheet. These field names must match the database field names exactly.

2. Highlight the names and the row beneath them.

3. Select the Data-Set Criteria option.

Figure 11-6 shows an example of highlighting the criteria range.

Sets the highlighted range as the criteria range and makes it available for use. You only need to create the criteria range once. ☐

220

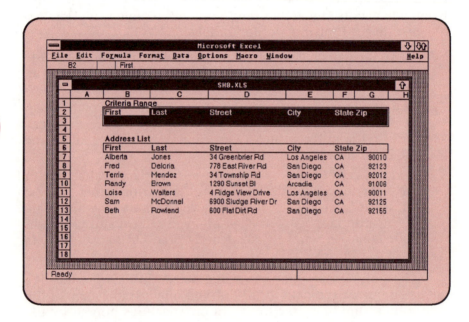

Figure 11-6.   Highlighting the criteria range.

Finding Records with the Criteria Range

You are now ready to use the criteria range to find database records. Simply enter the data you want to match in the row below the field names. For example, to find all people who live in San Diego, enter `San Diego` under the City heading as shown in Figure 11-7.

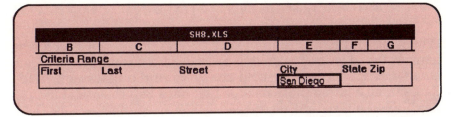

Figure 11-7. *Enter the criteria under the headings.*

You can enter criteria for any of the fields to narrow the search. You can also use the wild card and logical operators in your criteria. When the criteria are entered, leave the cell pointer in the criteria range and then select the Data-Find command. Excel highlights the first matching record in the database. Figure 11-8 shows an example.

221

	B	C	D	E	F	G	H	I
6	First	Last	Street	City	State	Zip		
7	Alberta	Jones	34 Greenbrier Rd	Los Angeles	CA	90010		
8	Fred	Deloria	778 East River Rd	San Diego	CA	92123		
9	Terrie	Mendez	34 Township Rd	San Diego	CA	92012		
10	Randy	Brown	1290 Sunset Bl	Arcadia	CA	91006		
11	Loise	Walters	4 Ridge View Drive	Los Angeles	CA	90011		
12	Sam	McDonnel	6900 Sludge River Dr	San Diego	CA	92125		
13	Beth	Rowlend	600 Flat Dirt Rd	San Diego	CA	92155		

Find (Use direction keys to view records)

Figure 11-8. *Excel finds the first matching record.*

You can now use the ↑ and ↓ keys to view other matching records. Press Esc to return to normal worksheet operation.

Extending Matching Criteria

When you add more criteria to the criteria range, you effectively narrow the possible matching records. For example, you can enter San Diego in the City field and Brown in the Last Name field. Rather than finding those records that have San Diego in the City field, Excel must find records with San Diego in the City field AND Brown in the Last Name field. Fewer records will match both criteria. By making entries in multiple fields of the criteria range, you can create this kind of *AND* condition for the criteria.

But suppose you want to find records that have San Diego in the City Field *OR* Brown in the Last Name field? In other words, a record will match if it meets *either* condition. OR conditions actually extend the number of possible matching records. To enter an OR condition for criteria, enter the different pieces of data on different rows under the criteria headings. An example would look like Figure 11-9.

222

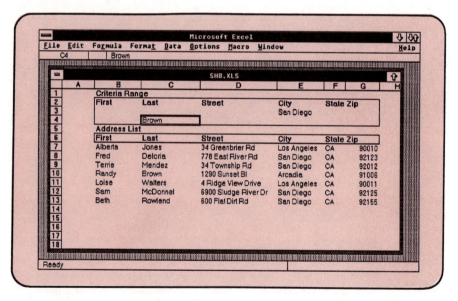

Figure 11-9. **Entering OR conditions in the extract range.**

Notice that the two criteria entries appear on different rows beneath the criteria headings. Also, the criteria range has been extended to include an extra row of values. You must highlight all rows and use the Data-Set Criteria command to include all rows in the criteria range. Figure 11-10 shows another example. In Figure 11-10's example, all records with San Diego or Arcadia in the City field will match.

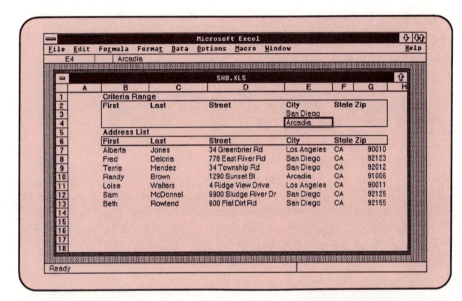

Figure 11-10. Matching San Diego or Arcadia in the City field.

223

Deleting Records in Batches

You can delete records one at a time from the database using the data form. You can also delete records by deleting the worksheet rows that contain the undesired records. But you might find the need to delete a batch of records that match certain criteria. For example, you could remove records that have a particular date in them. To delete a batch of records at one time, enter the appropriate criteria into the criteria range. This criteria should locate only those records you want to remove. Next, select the Data-Delete command. After confirming the deletion, Excel removes the records that match your criteria.

Extracting Records

Extracting records from a database is an extension of finding records using a criteria range. But instead of highlighting records, Excel duplicates the matching records and places them in a list. You need to prepare three elements to extract records from a database:

▶ The active database range

▶ The criteria range to match the database range

▶ The extract range

The *extract range* is the area of the worksheet where you would like to place the duplicated records. The extract range should be placed below the database records on the worksheet, and it should begin with a row of headings as shown in Figure 11-11. The headings you enter in the extract range must match the field names in the database exactly for the extract to work properly. You can simply copy the headings from the database range.

224

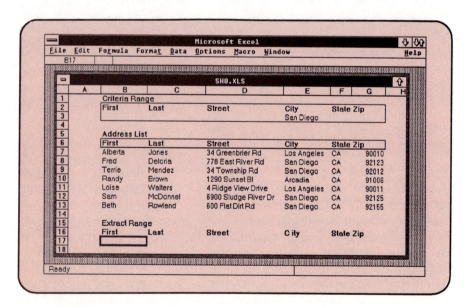

Figure 11-11.   An example extract range below the database range.

The next step is to enter the desired criteria into the criteria range. This will determine which records are extracted. For example, we'll just use San Diego in the City field to extract all records with this data. Now highlight the headings of the extract range as shown in Figure 11-12 and select the Data-Extract command. Excel will ask if you want to extract Unique Records Only. Press Enter at this message to select all matching records. Or, if the database may contain duplicates of some records and you do not want to extract every duplicate, press U to check the unique records only option. Next, Excel will place the records that match the search criteria into the extract range below the highlighted headings. Figure 11-13 shows a completed extract procedure.

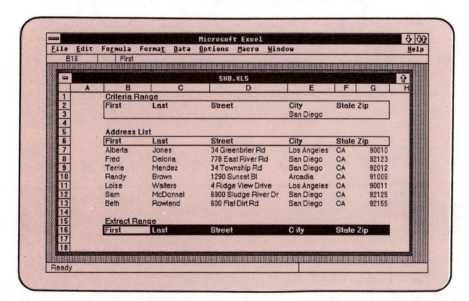

Figure 11-12.   Highlighting the extract range before extracting.

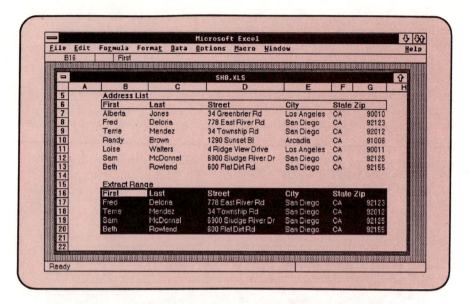

Figure 11-13. *The completed extract procedure.*

⊘ **Caution:** Make sure that no worksheet data appears below the extract range. When Excel extracts the records and places them into this range, it erases all data below the range.

The procedure for extracting database records is summarized in the following Quick Steps.

 Extracting Database Records

1. Create the database and criteria ranges as described earlier. Be sure that the criteria range has been activated with the Data-Set Criteria command.

2. Enter all search criteria into the criteria range.

Designates the records that will be selected.

3. Copy the headings from the database range to a new area below the database. Do not use an area that contains information below it.

Creates the extract range headings and defines the worksheet area where the extracted records will be copied.

4. Highlight the copied extract range headings.

5. Select the Data-Extract command.

Excel responds by asking if you want to select Unique Records Only.

6. To extract all matching records, press Enter. To extract only one copy of each matching record, press U to check the unique records only option, then press Enter.

Copies of the extracted records will be placed in the extract range.

227

When you extract records from the database, you don't have to duplicate every field in each record. In other words, you can extract portions of the matching records. In the example in Figure 11-11, you might want to extract only the First Name and Last Name fields for the San Diego records. This lets you create specific lists of information by extracting from a database. To select specific fields for the extract procedure, simply list in the extract range only those fields you want extracted. Figure 11-14 shows an example.

Notice that in Figure 11-14 the two extract fields are also in a different order than their appearance in database range. This is perfectly okay. Excel will extract the fields you specify, in the order you specify. Figure 11-15 shows the extracted records using the two extract fields.

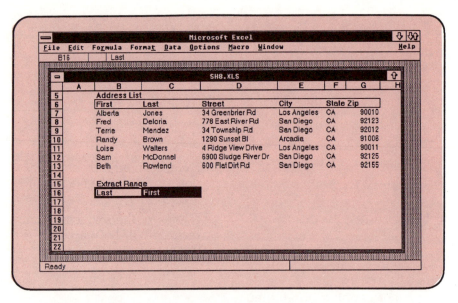

Figure 11-14.   Extracting a limited number of fields from the matching records.

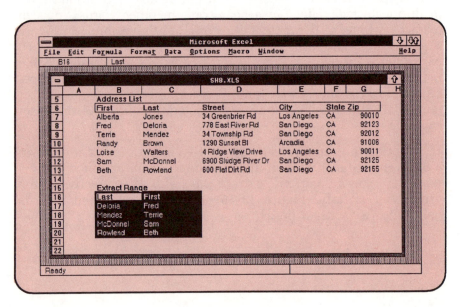

Figure 11-15.   The extracted records.

> **Tip:** If you have any problems extracting data, you may have entered the fields incorrectly. Try copying them from the database range to be sure they match.

What You've Learned

This chapter covered details about finding and extracting database records. You learned how to use the data form and a criteria range to find records. The criteria range offers several advantages over the data form, even if the criteria range is a bit more complicated to use. Here are some important points covered in this chapter:

▶ Use the Criteria button on the data form to enter search criteria for locating records in the database.

▶ Enter any data into the appropriate fields in the criteria form, then press Alt-N for the Find Next command. This locates the next record in the database that matches the data you specified.

▶ You can use wild cards and logical operators in the search criteria to increase the power of your searches.

▶ A criteria range consists of the field names, plus one or more blank rows beneath them. You must set the criteria range with the Data-Set Criteria command.

▶ Specify the criteria under each heading in the criteria range. Data on the same row narrows the possible matching records by establishing AND conditions. Data on different rows extends possible matching records by establishing OR conditions.

▶ To extract records, duplicate the desired fields under the database range. This is called the extract range. Highlight these fields and use the Data-Extract command to extract records that match your criteria.

229

Excel Macros

In This Chapter

- ▶ *Understanding macros*
- ▶ *Creating a macro*
- ▶ *Using the macro recorder*
- ▶ *Saving and running macros*
- ▶ *Adding more macros to the worksheet*
- ▶ *Running macros from a menu*

This chapter shows you how to tap into Excel's macro powers. Macros are useful for automating tasks in worksheets. You can create macros that operate on any worksheet you like, or you can create macros that work only on specific worksheets. First, the chapter shows you how to create a macro using the macro recording feature in Excel. Then viewing and editing the macro is covered. Finally, the chapter teaches how to save the macro for future use so you can run the macro at any time.

Understanding Macros

A macro is a small program that controls Excel. The macro performs commands, selects data and generally does anything you would do within Excel—but without your help. Using a macro is like having "autopilot" for Excel. Anything you can do within Excel, a macro can do automatically. You can rest your fingers and let the macro take over. Often, macros are used to perform repetitious tasks, such as formatting data or entering commonly-used labels like month names.

But if macros merely repeat things that you can do yourself, what good are they? Well, for one thing, macros perform tasks much faster than you do. A macro can issue five or six different formatting commands in the blink of an eye. In fact, you probably cannot distinguish between the various commands being issued. Another advantage to a macro is that it repeats the same task over and over without error. If you were to repeat a series of commands over and over, chances are you'd make mistakes occasionally. As you experiment with macros, you'll discover other advantages they offer.

Just because macros are similar to programs, don't let the idea of creating a macro scare you off. Macros are very simple to create and use. While they offer powerful advantages for your worksheets, Excel makes them very easy to create. You don't need to know anything about programming. In fact, Excel does most of the work for you.

Creating a Macro

Excel lets you create macros by recording commands like a tape recorder. Simply turn the recorder on, perform the commands you want the macro to duplicate, then turn the recorder off. Once the "recording" is made, you can play it over and over again by typing a simple command. Everything you do while the recorder is on will be repeated by the macro when you "play" it.

Of course, Excel does not record the macro using an actual tape recorder. Instead, Excel records a series of macro commands that "describe" the tasks you request. For every action you take, Excel enters an equivalent command into the macro recording. You can then save this recording for future use. Following are the Quick Steps used to record a macro.

Q **Recording a Macro**

1. With the desired worksheet in view, select the Macro Record command.

   This brings up the dialog box shown in Figure 12-1. Excel suggests a name and shortcut key for the macro, but you can replace these as described in the next two steps.

2. Enter a descriptive name for the macro to replace the default name Record1. The name should not contain spaces. Press Tab when finished.

233

3. Enter a one-character shortcut key for the macro. Later, you'll use this character with the Ctrl key to play back the macro. It's a good idea to use a shortcut key that reminds you of the macro's purpose. Press Enter when finished.

4. Perform any commands you want to record in the macro. When finished, select the command Macro-Stop Recorder.

   Your actions have been translated into macro commands and recorded onto a blank macro worksheet. ☐

▶ **Note:** When entering shortcut keys, remember that Excel distinguishes between upper- and lowercase letters. For instance, you can use the key R for one macro and r for another.

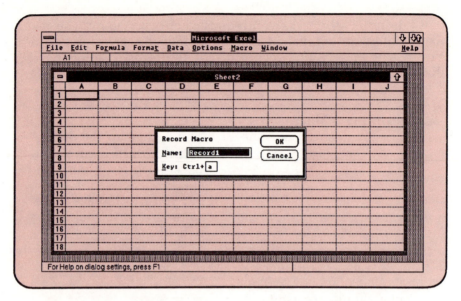

Figure 12-1.   Excel asks you to name the macro before recording.

Let's try creating a sample macro. This macro will enter the month names at the top of your worksheet. Use the File-New command to open a new worksheet. Select the Macro-Record command. Enter the macro name MONTHS into the dialog box. Press Tab and enter m as the shortcut key. Press Enter when finished.

You are now recording the macro. Move the pointer to cell A4 and begin typing the month names in this row, pressing Tab after each one. Select the Macro-Stop Recorder command when you have finished typing the names to complete the macro.

 Tip: Remember that Excel distinguishes between upper- and lowercase letters for macro shortcut keys.

Viewing the Macro

Now that you have finished a test macro, let's take a look at the recording. While you were entering the information for the macro,

Excel opened a macro worksheet and recorded all your macro commands onto this worksheet. The macro worksheet appears behind your worksheet. To look at the macro worksheet, select its name (Macro1) from the Window menu. If you followed the previous steps for creating a sample macro, the macro worksheet should look like Figure 12-2.

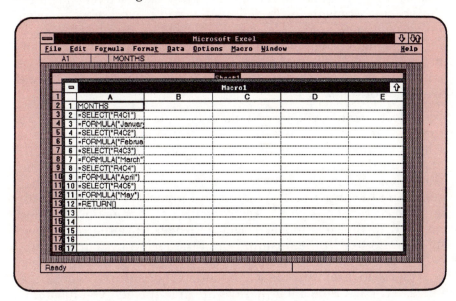

Figure 12-2.   The sample macro.

235

First of all, notice that the macro worksheet looks very much like a regular worksheet. The macro commands that duplicate your actions are listed in column A. The macro begins with the name you specified, and then the commands appear under the name. If you examine these commands, you'll probably find that they are fairly easy to understand because they are similar to the actions you recorded. Another thing to notice is that the macro ends with the RETURN() command. All macros begin with a name and end with the RETURN() command. (Well, there are a few exceptions, but they are fairly advanced.)

Finally, notice that each macro command, except for the name, begins with an = sign. Because Excel's macro commands are considered to be formulas on a macro worksheet, Excel automatically enters the macro commands as formulas by including the = sign. You'll see why this syntax is important later in this chapter.

Editing the Macro

With the macro worksheet in view on the screen, you can make changes to the macro using Excel's editing commands, which were discussed in Chapter 5. You can remove macro commands, edit the specific contents of a cell in the macro worksheet or even insert new commands into the middle of the macro. Of course, making some changes will require knowledge of the macro commands. Specific commands that relate to actions you want are described in the *Excel Functions and Macros* manual that came with the software.

Most likely, you'll occasionally want to "clean up" a recorded macro by removing stray commands. For example, if you make mistakes while recording a macro, those mistakes will appear in the macro and will be repeated each time you run the macro. Or, you might make an incorrect entry, then add another command to correct it. The macro will repeat the incorrect entry and the correction each time. The result will be fine, but there is no need to repeat a mistake over and over. In either case, you might want to edit the mistake out of the macro by removing the cells containing the incorrect macro commands. You probably will need to examine the commands to determine where the mistake occurs. Remember to save the macro when you have finished editing.

Saving the Macro

To save a macro, you must save the macro worksheet. Since macro worksheets are similar to standard worksheets, simply use the File-Save command as described in Chapter 3. You can choose any name for the macro and specify any directory path for the file. However, avoid giving the file an extension because Excel will apply the .XLM extension to indicate that the file contains a macro.

Once the macro is saved, you can close the macro worksheet without losing the macro. Open the macro worksheet again to use the macro in the future. The File-Open command will open a macro worksheet. If you open a macro worksheet by typing the macro file name (as opposed to highlighting its name in the file listing), then you should remember to include the .XLM extension.

Playing (Running) the Macro

Once you have recorded a macro, you can run it at any time. Make sure a worksheet and the macro worksheet are open. Then simply press Ctrl along with the shortcut key you specified for the macro. The steps you recorded will be repeated automatically by Excel.

Keep in mind, however, that the same conditions should exist when you run a macro as existed when you created the macro. For example, if you created the macro that enters month names at the top of a worksheet, which you would normally do when you open a new worksheet, you should run the macro when opening a new worksheet or when a worksheet has no information at the top. The macro commands *could* produce errors if the wrong worksheet is open. If you were to run the macro on a worksheet that contains information at the top, some information might be replaced. If you try to run the macro when no worksheet is present, the macro would simply not work.

To run the sample macro we created to enter the months at the top of a worksheet, open the macro worksheet and a new worksheet. The worksheet should be in view. Press Ctrl-m to run the macro on the worksheet. The month names will appear in the same cells where you entered them when you created the macro. You can use this macro on any worksheet you like. Just make sure that the macro worksheet and the desired worksheet are open.

237

Macro Cell References

If you ran the sample macro on a sample worksheet, you saw that it repeated your recorded keystrokes and actions exactly. The same information was entered into the same cells. Each time you run the macro, it will enter the month names into row 4.

But what if you wanted the macro to enter the month names in any row you specify, rather than row 4 all the time? When you record the macro, you could tell the macro to enter the month names beginning at the current cell position. The entries would be made relative to the cell pointer.

The ability to specify where a macro should place information each time it's run is known as *relative referencing*. Using relative referencing, all movement commands are recorded relative to the pointer's position at the time you begin recording. For example, with normal recording on, if the pointer is in cell A1 when you begin recording the macro and you move the pointer down to cell A2 and enter January, the macro will translate your action as "enter January in cell A2." Each time you run the macro, Excel will enter January in cell A2. If you use relative referencing, however, the macro will record the same action as "move down one cell and type January." When you run the macro another time, Excel will "move down one cell" from the location of the pointer, wherever it happens to be when you run the macro.

Using relative referencing is easy. Just use the Macro-Relative Record command immediately after turning the recorder on and naming the macro. Try relative referencing by creating a macro similar to the sample macro we made to enter the month names into a worksheet. After you turn the macro recorder on, enter a name and a shortcut key, select the Macro-Relative Record command. Place the pointer in cell A4, then type each month name followed by the Tab key. Select the Macro-Stop Recorder command. The new macro will look like Figure 12-3.

If you compare this macro to the first one we created, you'll notice that the cell references are entered quite differently. The new entries are relative references in the macro. When you run this macro on a new worksheet, the month names will begin at the pointer location and continue across the row. You can try to run your new sample macro, placing the pointer at various loca-

238

tions in a worksheet and entering Ctrl plus the shortcut key you selected.

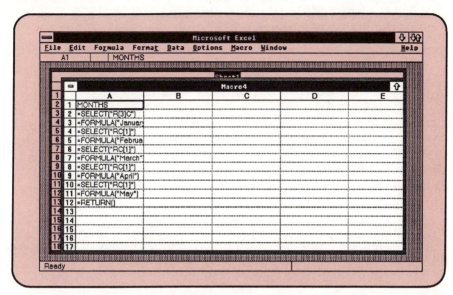

Figure 12-3.   The sample macro after recording with Macro-Relative Record.

Adding a Second Macro

You now have the complete procedure for creating, saving and using macros in your worksheets. You can continue to create macro after macro using the techniques presented. Each macro you create will be recorded in its own macro worksheet. You might find yourself accumulating more macro worksheets than you care to. And since a macro cannot be run unless its macro worksheet is open, this could mean opening several macro worksheets just to have your most useful macros active at the same time.

To avoid macro worksheet overload, Excel lets you place more than one macro on a single macro worksheet. Placing two macros in a single worksheet is especially useful when the macros will be used at the same time. For example, two macros may relate to the same worksheet or a set of general macros might be handy to have available to work on any worksheet. Adding a second macro to an existing macro worksheet is slightly different than creating the first macro. There are, in fact, two ways to create additional macros. The following sections discuss creating additional macros by hand and by using a variation of the macro recorder.

Entering a Second Macro by Hand

One way to create a second macro is to enter the macro commands by hand onto the macro worksheet. This technique is convenient when the macros are very simple (requiring only one or two commands) or very complex (requiring special macro constructs). In this book, we'll only examine how to enter a very simple macro by hand.

240

The components of the macro are the name, the commands and the RETURN function at the end. Following are the Quick Steps.

Q Hand-Entering a Simple Macro

1. Bring the worksheet for the first macro into view on the screen by selecting its name from the Window menu.

2. Position the cell pointer in cell that will begin the new macro. Use a cell under the existing macro so that if you need to insert or delete rows from the first macro, you won't disturb the second macro. Enter the name of the macro in this cell.

   Figure 12-4 shows an example.

3. Press the ↓ key and enter the macro commands in order down the column. Remember to enter the commands with = signs at

   If you enter the commands in lower-case letters, Excel converts them to upper-case when you press ↓ or Enter. An improperly

the beginning. Conclude the macro with the RETURN( ) command.

4. Save the macro worksheet to keep the macro you've added.

entered command will not be converted to uppercase letters. Figure 12-5 shows an example of this stage.

☐

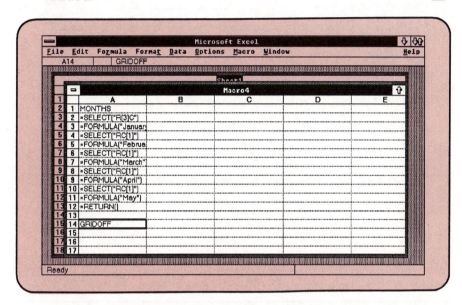

Figure 12-4.   *Selecting the first cell of a second macro.*

241

You have now entered the macro, but it's not ready to be used yet. Before you can use the macro, you must activate it as described under the heading *Activating the Macro* later in this chapter. But first, let's examine another way to add a second macro to the macro worksheet.

When you create a hand-entered macro, you obviously need to know the specific commands that relate to the actions you want. Some of the more common macro commands available in Excel are described in Appendix B. The *Excel Functions and Macros* manual lists all the macro commands. For this reason, you might find it easier to record the second macro using the procedure described next.

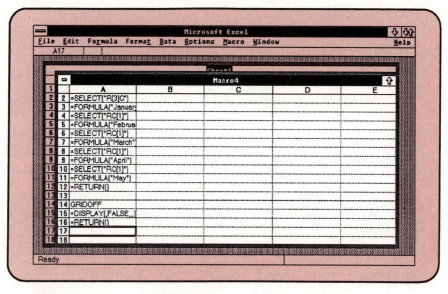

Figure 12-5. **Entering the macro commands.**

Recording a Second Macro

The second way to create additional macros on the same worksheet is to use the macro recorder, but you can't use it exactly as
you did for the first macro. There is a slight variation. You must
first tell Excel where on the worksheet you would like the
recorded macro commands to be placed. Following are the
Quick Steps.

 Recording a Second Macro

1. Bring the worksheet for the
   first macro into view on
   the screen by selecting its
   name from the Window
   menu.

2. Position the cell pointer in
   the cell that will begin the
   macro, preferably a cell
   below other macros in the
   worksheet. Enter the name
   of the macro in this cell.

3. Select the Macro-Set Recorder command.	Activates the current cell as the first cell of the new macro.
4. Bring the desired worksheet into view using the Window menu, or open a new worksheet. This is the worksheet you will use to record your actions.	
5. Select the Macro-Start Recorder command. (This is not the Macro-Record command used to create the first macro.)	Begins the recorder and places all subsequent macro commands into the macro worksheet at the location you specified. Remember that you can also use the Macro-Relative Record command to record relative references.
6. Perform any actions you want to record, then select the Macro-Stop Recorder command when finished.	□

243

After recording a second macro on an existing macro worksheet, you can view the macro worksheet again to see the new commands. They appear in the column at the location you specified. Save the changes to the macro worksheet. As with a hand-entered macro, the recorded macro is not yet ready to be used. You must activate it first.

Activating the Macro

Once you have entered or recorded an additional macro on a macro worksheet, you must activate the additional macro before it can be used. Activating the macro consists of naming the macro (usually with the same name you entered in the first cell of the macro) and specifying a shortcut key. Remember that each of the macros should have a different name and shortcut key when they appear on the same worksheet and are going to be used at the same time. Use the following Quick Steps for activating a macro.

Activating the Macro

1. Bring the macro worksheet into view on the screen, then place the pointer in the first cell of the macro you want to activate. This cell contains the macro's name.

2. Select the Formula-Define Name command.

The Formula-Define Name dialog box appears on the screen. The name of the macro (as entered in the current cell) is already displayed in the dialog box. Figure 12-6 shows an example.

244

3. Verify that the name is correct and then press Alt-C to select the Command option.

Tells Excel that you are naming a macro.

4. Press Tab and enter the desired shortcut key for the macro. Use any single character. Press Enter when finished.

The macro is now active, and you can save the macro worksheet again.

Once you have activated the macro, you can use it anytime the macro worksheet is open. Filling up a macro worksheet this way helps you avoid creating too many macro worksheets for your needs.

What You've Learned

Macros are a powerful and time-saving tool when using worksheets. You can use macros to automate lengthy tasks that require several commands, including changing fonts, setting print areas,

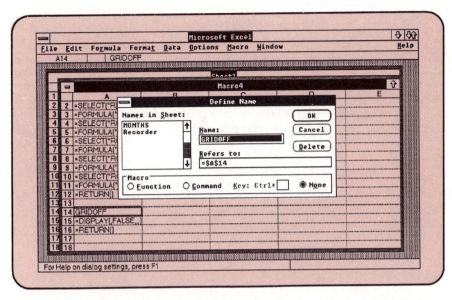

Figure 12-6.   Naming the macro.

setting up printer specifications, formatting data and more. Appendix B lists some of the more common macro commands. Following are some points to remember from this chapter:

▶ Macros are useful for automating repetitious tasks or for combining a series of actions into a single macro command.

▶ You can create a macro by recording your own actions. Do this with the Macro-Record command.

▶ When you record a macro, Excel adds a macro worksheet to the screen and translates your actions into macro commands. The macro worksheet can be saved for future use.

▶ You can run a macro by pressing Ctrl with the shortcut key you specify for the macro.

▶ To run a macro, the macro worksheet must be open. However, it can be behind the desired worksheet.

▶ You can change a macro by altering the entries in the macro worksheet with basic worksheet editing commands.

▶ You can add a second macro to the macro worksheet by using the Macro-Set Recorder and Macro-Start Recorder commands.

▶ After adding a second macro, use the Formula-Define name command to activate it. Activating a macro makes it available for use and lets you specify the shortcut key that will run it.

Worksheet Functions

Chapter 7 explained the uses of worksheet functions and showed examples of some functions in action. If you've read Chapter 7, you have a basic understanding of the purposes of functions and how they work. This appendix provides a listing of several more Excel functions and simple examples of each. Check Chapter 7 for more details about some of these functions.

Each function is listed along with an indication of where arguments should be included.

Mathematical Functions

Mathematical functions perform general mathematical operations, such as finding the absolute value of a number or rounding a number. Excel can also perform some logarithmic functions. Following are the mathematical functions provided in Excel.

ABS(value)

The ABS function calculates the absolute value of a number. That is, this function gives you a number without indicating whether it's positive or negative. For example, the absolute value of -52 is 52. Enter any number, formula or cell reference for the value argument.

Examples of the ABS function and its results are:

= **ABS(-25)**   25

= **ABS(A5)**, where A5   25
contains -25

INT(value)

The INT function rounds a number *down* to the nearest integer, resulting in a positive or negative number without decimal values. For example, the INT value of 24.87 is 24. Enter a number, formula or cell reference as the argument.

Examples of the INT function and its results are:

= **INT(24.55)**   24

= **INT(A5)**, where A5   24
contains 24.55

MOD(dividend,divisor)

The MOD function calculates the *modulus* of a divisor and a dividend. The modulus is the remainder after a divisor is divided by the dividend. For example, 26 divided by 5 equals 5, with a remainder of 1. So the modulus of 26 and 5 is 1.

The *dividend* and *divisor* can be any number or expression resulting in a number. The divisor cannot be zero.

Examples of the MOD function and its results are:

= **MOD(16,4)**   0

= **MOD(A5,A6)**, where   1
A5 contains 26 and A6
contains 5

PI()

This function can be used in place of the value *pi*. Excel calculates *pi* to 14 decimal places. Be sure to include the empty parentheses, even though there is no argument for this function.

An example of the PI function and its result is:

=**PI( )*A5^2**, where A5   28.27
contains 3

PRODUCT(value,value,value . . .)

The PRODUCT function calculates the product of the specified values. The product function multiplies the values to arrive at a total using the following formula: value * value * value * . . .

References to blank cells or cells containing text are ignored by the PRODUCT function. Enter any value, cell reference or formula as each of the values, or enter a range to specify the entire list of values. You may enter as many values as needed.

Examples of the PRODUCT function and its results are:

=**PRODUCT(3,5,2)**   30

=**PRODUCT(A1:A3)**,   30
where A1:A3 contain
the values 3, 5 and 2

=**PRODUCT(SALES)**,   30
where SALES is the
name of the range
A1:A3

ROUND(value,precision)

The ROUND function rounds a value to a specified number of places. Although you can use the Format-Number command and Excel's number formats to round a number, the number rounded is only *displayed* as a rounded number. Any calculations that use the number are made with the entire, unrounded value. On the other hand, the ROUND function permanently changes the value of a number to a rounded value. Enter the number to be rounded as the *value*, and the desired number of places as the *precision*.

Examples of the ROUND function and its results are:

=**ROUND(24.55,1)**   24.6

=**ROUND(A5,2)**, where   24.56
A5 contains 24.5589

Statistical Functions

250

Statistical functions work on groups of numbers. Common statistical functions include calculating the average of a group, finding the minimum and maximum value from a group, and adding the numbers in a group. Statistical functions can get much more advanced than this, such as standard deviation and sample statistics calculations.

AVERAGE(range)

AVERAGE calculates the mean average of a group of numbers. Enter the range containing the numbers you want to average. This function interprets text as values of zero and skips blank cells.

An example of the AVERAGE function and its result is:

=**AVERAGE(A1:A5)**,   13.4
where A1:A5 contains
the values 3, 4, 25, 30
and 5

COUNT(range) and COUNTA(range)

These two functions count the number of cells in a range. The COUNT function counts only numeric values, and the COUNTA function counts all cells that are not blank. Enter any range as the argument.

For example, let's say the range A1:A5 contains the following values:

A1:	3
A2:	Text
A3:	25
A4:	(Blank)
A5:	0

Using the above values, results of using the COUNT and COUNTA functions are:

=**COUNT(A1:A5)**	3
=**COUNTA(A1:A5)**	4

MIN(range) and MAX(range)

The MAX and MIN functions return the maximum and minimum values in a range of cells. The argument can be a range of cells, random cell references, formulas, constant values or some combination of these values.

Examples of these functions and the results are:

MAX(A1:A5), where A1:A5 contains 3, 4, 20, 25 and 10	25

MAX(A1,25,   25
C23*3,"green"), where
A1 contains 5 and C23
contains 3

SUM(range)

The SUM function calculates the total of a group of cells, which can consist of a range reference or a list of individual cells or values. A range can be in a row, column or block. If you want to add values that are not in a row or a column, enter them individually as a list.

Examples of the SUM function and its results are:

252

=**SUM(A1:A5)**, where   25
A1:A5 contains 3, 6, 2,
5 and 9

=**SUM(3,6,A3,A4+2,9)**,   27
where A3 contains 2
and A4 contains 5

Financial Functions

Financial functions are used for various financial calculations involving interest rates, loan terms, present values and future values. Financial functions are essential for performing in-depth financial analysis of purchases, investments and cash flow.

DDB(cost,salvage,life,period,factor)

The DDB function calculates depreciation using the double declining balance method, which accelerates the rate of depreciation early in the life of an asset. When the asset's book value depreciates to the salvage value, depreciation stops.

Enter values (cell references or constant values) for the initial cost, the salvage value, the life of the asset and the period for which depreciation is being calculated. The life and period should both be in the same time measurement, such as years, months or days. Optionally, you can enter a factor for the rate of depreciation. If you do not enter a *factor*, the function assumes a factor of 2 (i.e., double declining).

For example, let's say you are depreciating an asset over a 10-year life and want to calculate the depreciation in year 10. The cost (10,000) is in cell A5 and the salvage value (500) is in cell A6. The formula with the DDB function and the result of the calculation would be as follows:

=DDB(A5,A6,10,10)   268.44

FV(interest rate,periods,payment   **253**
 amount,present value,type)

FV calculates the future value of an investment, after payments have been made at a particular rate over a particular amount of time. The function finds the total dollar value of an investment after the investment has matured. Enter the *interest rate* as the periodic rate (usually a monthly or yearly rate). The *periods* argument contains the number of periods that the investment is active. You should use the same type of period for this argument and the interest rate (in months, years, etc.). The payment *amount* is the amount of each payment to the investment and represents a regular amount. The *present value* is the starting value of the investment. The *type* indicates whether payments are made at the beginning or end of the period. Entering 1 indicates the beginning and 0 indicates the end. Of course, any of these arguments can be cell references.

Remember that cash paid out must be shown as a negative number and interest or cash received is a positive number. Therefore, if you are calculating the future value of a savings account, the present value (amount deposited) and the payment amount (monthly deposits) will be negative numbers because they are "paid out" to the investment.

Consider this example of a formula with the FV function and its result:

```
=FV(12%/12,                    29042.38
120,-125,0,1)
```

Notice that the annual interest rate is converted to a monthly (periodic) rate using the formula 12%/12, and that the term and payment values reflect the same type of period (months). The result shows that you will have $29,042.38 after ten years (120 months) of depositing $125 monthly at a 12% annual interest rate.

IPMT(rate,period,periods,present value,future value,type)

254

This function calculates the interest paid for a particular payment given the interest rate, the number of periods in the term and the present value. Specify the period for which you want to determine the interest being paid. The type determines whether payments are made at the beginning (1) of the period or at the end (0).

NPER(rate,payment,present value,future value,type)

This function calculates the number of payments required to pay off a loan at a given interest rate. You can also use this function to calculate the number of periods required for a savings plan to build to a specific future value, based on a present value and an interest rate. Enter the periodic interest rate, the payment amount, the present value of the investment, the future value of the investment and a type value of 0 or 1. A 1 indicates that payments occur at the beginning of the period. A 0 indicates that payments occur at the end of the period.

NPV(rate,range)

This function calculates the present value of a series of cash flow transactions. The *rate* is the periodic interest rate of an investment of equivalent risk and the *range* is the range of cells containing the cash incomes or outflows. If you are the investor or lender, remember that the loan paid out will be negative and the payments in are positive. If the result is a positive number, the investment can be considered a good one.

PMT(rate,periods,present value,future value,type)

This function calculates the payment amount required for an investment to be paid off given a specific term and interest rate. The interest rate should be the rate for each payment period. For example, if you want to calculate a weekly payment amount, the rate should be a weekly rate (the annual rate divided by 52).

PPMT(rate,period,periods,present value,future value,type)

255

This function calculates the amount of principal being paid during any of the payment periods, given the periodic interest rate and number of periods. Chapter 7 shows a complete example of using this function to view the principal amount of each payment.

RATE(periods,payment,present value,future value,type,guess)

The RATE function calculates the interest rate required for a present value to become a greater value given a particular number of payment periods. This function is useful for determining the interest rate you are being charged on a loan, such as an auto loan. When you are quoted a price and a monthly payment amount, you can figure out the interest rate using the RATE function.

Excel calculates the interest rate using a *guess* entered into the formula. Start by leaving the guess argument blank to tell Excel to try the calculation on its own. If Excel fails to calculate a correct interest rate (indicated by the #NUM statement in the cell), enter a guess on the interest rate. Remember to enter the payment amount as a negative number if you are the investor and the present and future values as negative if you are the borrower.

SLN(cost,salvage,life)

The SLN function calculates depreciation using the straight line method. This method accelerates depreciation at a constant rate for the entire life of the asset. Enter the initial cost, the salvage value and the life of the asset (in years).

An example of the SLN function and its result is:

=**SLN(A5,A6,10),**   950.00
where A5 contains
10,000 and A6 contains
500

256

SYD(cost,salvage,life,period)

This is a third depreciation method called the sum of the years' digits method. Enter the initial cost, the salvage value, the life of the asset and the period for which depreciation is calculated.

You can use the SYD function to calculate depreciation in year 10 when the asset has a 10-year life, cell A5 contains 10,000 and cell A6 contains 500. The formula and its result are as follows :

=**SYD(A5,A6,10,10)**   172.73

Lookup Functions

Lookup functions search for values within tables or lists. Each lookup function uses a different method for searching and returning values. You'll find each method suited for a particular task. Any time your worksheet uses tables to hold values, such as tax tables or price tables, you can employ a lookup function for added power in the application.

HLOOKUP(value,range,row offset)
VLOOKUP(value,range,column offset)

These two lookup functions search for values in tables based on a *lookup value*, the value you are trying to match. For example, a tax table contains tax rates based on income. Income is the lookup value. VLOOKUP searches vertically in a column of values, then returns a corresponding value from the table. HLOOKUP searches horizontally in a row of values, then returns a corresponding value from the table.

The *value* can be any valid number or text string (or expression resulting in a valid number or string, including formulas and cell references). The *range* is the worksheet range containing the table. The *row offset* and *column offset* determine the row or column with the value for the lookup function to return. The VLOOKUP function takes the lookup value and looks down the first column of the table for a match. When a match is found, the function moves across the table along the row with the matched value, to return the value in the offset column specified in the formula. Chapter 7 shows a complete example of using this function. (HLOOKUP searches across to match the lookup value, then down a column to return a value from the appropriate offset row.)

257

If the search variable is numeric, then the values in the lookup column (or row) should be numeric. Moreover, these values should be in ascending order. If the lookup column is not in ascending order, the functions may return incorrect values. Excel searches the lookup column until it finds a direct match. If a direct match cannot be found, the closest value smaller than the search variable is used. Therefore, if a lookup value is greater than all values in the table, the last value in the table is used because it's the largest. If the lookup value is smaller than all values in the table, then the function returns the error: #VALUE!

If the lookup range within the specified table range contains text strings, then the search variable must also be a text string. In such cases, the lookup function must be able to find an exact match for the specified information, including upper- and lower-case letters. If no match is found the function will return the error: #VALUE! The data in the table (that is, the value to be returned) can be numeric values or text.

Logical Functions

Logical functions are used to create logical tests. A test enables a formula to make a decision based on particular data. A test may determine if a value is greater than 25, and the formula making the test can perform one function if true and another if false. The most common and useful logical function is the IF function, which allows you to develop several kinds of tests based on the operators used in the test statement. IF is often combined with other logical functions to create more specific tests.

IF(condition,value if true,value if false)

258

The IF function tests that a condition is true or false. If the condition proves true, one value is returned. If the condition proves false, another value is returned. To prove a condition true or false requires a relational operator. Excel offers several:

>   is greater than

<   is less than

=   is equal to

>=   is greater than or equal to

<=   is less than or equal to

<>   is not equal to

In the following example, you can substitute any of these operators for the one given:

IF(A1 = A2,"Right","Wrong")

If the value of A1 is equal to that of A2, then the formula will return Right. Otherwise, the formula will return Wrong. The *value if true* and the *value if false* can be any constant value, cell reference or formula. Chapter 7 provides a complete example of using the IF function.

ISBLANK(cell)

This function tests whether a cell is blank. If the specified cell is blank, a value of TRUE is returned, otherwise, FALSE is returned. The referenced cell can be any valid cell in the worksheet. The ISBLANK function is commonly used along with the IF function to test for a blank cell, then perform some action based on the outcome. For example, you can use ISBLANK along with IF to print a message next to cells that need to be filled in, then remove the message once the data is entered. Here's that formula:

> =IF(ISBLANK(B5) = FALSE, "", "Please enter the amount in cell B5")

259

ISERR(cell)

This function tests whether a specified cell contains an error. If so, then a value of TRUE is returned. Otherwise, FALSE is returned. The ISERR function is commonly used along with the IF function to "trap" errors in the worksheet and allow control over the result of the error. Normally, any calculation that references a cell containing and error will cause #VALUE! or some other error message to be returned. But using the ISERR function, you can pinpoint the error. For example:

> =IF(ISERR(B5) = TRUE, "Invalid entry in cell B5", B5*B6)

This formula tests if the value of B5 is an error. If so, the phrase Invalid entry in cell B5 is returned. Otherwise, the desired calculation is performed.

Date/Time Functions

Date and time functions are used specifically for date and time math calculations and conversions. *Date math* and *time math* are the ability to calculate elapsed time, add time to a given date or time, or calculate the difference between two dates or times. The following functions are used for these calculations. For more information about date math, see Chapter 8.

DATEVALUE(text)

This function converts a text string into a valid date (in other words, a date serial number). The text string must contain data which is recognizable as a date. The function recognizes text entered in any of the date formats shown in the Format-Numbers command. You can specify any date from January 1, 1904 to February 6, 2040.

An example of the DATEVALUE function and its result is:

= **DATEVALUE (B5)**, where B5 contains 1/25/91	31801

The result, 31801, is the number of days between 1/1/04 and 1/25/91. You can format this date value using any of the date formats in the Format-Number command.

DAY(date)
MONTH(date)
YEAR(date)

These functions return the day, month or year corresponding to a specified date. The *date* variable can be any valid date entered as the number of days elapsed since January 1, 1904. The value can also be a reference to a cell containing a valid date, or it can be any date expression resulting in a valid date. These functions break a date into its various portions. For example, suppose cell B2 contains the date 2/24/90. Here are some examples of these functions and their results:

DAY(B2)	24
MONTH(B2)	2
YEAR(B2)	1990

NOW()

The NOW function pulls the current date and time from the DOS startup date and time. The value is returned as a number with a decimal value, as in 2245.2025. The integer part of this number represents the date (in "days elapsed" format) and the fractional part represents the time (in "time elapsed" format).

There is no argument for the function. You can simply format the value into a date using any of the date formats in the Format-Number menu, or you can format the value into a time using the time formats in the Format-Number menu. You can also use the TRUNC function to separate the two portions, as in =TRUNC(NOW()). This formula strips off the decimal portion of the date/time serial number, turning it into a date only. You can then format this date or use the DAY, MONTH and YEAR functions to split the value even further.

261

TIMEVALUE(text)

The TIMEVALUE function converts a text string into a valid time. The text string must be recognizable as a time entry. It should resemble any of the time formats in the Format-Number command. The result will be displayed in the "time elapsed" format, but can be formatted with the Format-Number command. Enter times as text strings by typing them in two or three parts (for example, 12:30 or 12:30:15) or by including the AM/PM (for example, 12:30:00 AM).

Here's an example of the function and its result:

> =**TIMEVALUE(B4)**,   0.9828125
> where B4 contains
> 11:35:15 PM

The numerical result can be formatted as the valid time 11:35:15 PM.

WEEKDAY(date)

This function returns the weekday name of any valid date as a value from 1 to 7. The value 1 equals Sunday, 2 equals Monday, and so on. To format this value as the appropriate day name, use the Format-Number command and specify the custom date format "dddd".

An example of this function and its result is:

=WEEKDAY(1/1/91)   6

The 6 can be formatted as the weekday name Thursday using the "dddd" format.

262

Macro Command Listing

This appendix provides information about some of the more common macro commands available in Excel. Some of these commands are automatically used by Excel when you record a macro and perform equivalent actions. Others, however, can only be used when you type a macro by hand. Some of these commands duplicate the menu options with which you have become familiar. Others are the equivalent of mouse or keyboard actions you can perform. There are many more commands available in Excel's macros. For a complete listing, see the *Functions and Macros* manual that comes with Excel.

Macro Cell and Range References

When you use the macro recorder, Excel takes care of entering cell and range references for you. However, if you attempt to type a macro by hand, you should know some basics about these references. Some of the macro commands listed in this appendix require that you enter a cell or range reference. One way to enter a cell reference is as a standard cell or range address, as in C5 or the range C5:G9. When used in a macro, these references refer to cells in the macro worksheet itself, not in the worksheet that might be active when you run the macro. For this reason, these references are used only for a macro's internal needs.

The most common need is to refer to the worksheet that is active when you run the macro. Since some macros can be useful for many different worksheets, you'll want to allow any worksheet to be active for the macro. To tell the macro to look for cell references in the currently active worksheet, simply enter an *exclamation* point in front of the reference, as in the following examples:

!C5

!C5:G9

!Sales

264

Another way to enter a reference is to use the *"RC"-style* address. This is a reference that applies to the current location of the pointer. This type of reference is used when you select the Macro-Relative Record command when recording macros. However, when programming a macro by hand, you must enter these relative references yourself. Some examples include:

"RC"

"R[1]C"

"R[4]C[-1]"

When you use this type of reference, you should include the quotation marks, making it a text string. The "RC" example refers to the current cell. The numbers in brackets move the reference either forward (positive) or backward (negative) by the indicated number of cells. Hence, the reference *R[1]C[1]* moves the pointer to the right and down one cell from the current position.

Remember that you can use any of these types of cell or range references whenever the macro command requests a reference. Following are some useful macro commands.

Duplicating Menu Options

Excel includes many macro commands that emulate standard menu commands. In fact, when you use a menu command while the macro recorder is on, Excel converts your actions to macro commands. Each menu command you select while recording becomes a command equivalent on the macro worksheet. Following are some of the more commonly used macro command equivalents for menu commands. These will be helpful when you want to edit a macro or type a macro by hand.

ALIGNMENT(type)

The ALIGNMENT command aligns information in the current cell, like the Formula-Alignment menu command. Enter a value from 1 to 5 as the type argument: 1 is General alignment, 2 is Left, 3 is Center, 4 is Right, 5 is Fill.

BORDER(outline,left,right,top,bottom,shade)

This command is equivalent to the Format-Border command. It creates a border line at the top, left side, right side or bottom of the active cell or range. It can also outline the range or fill it with a shade. Enter TRUE for any of the arguments to create a line and FALSE to remove it. Omit an argument to leave it as is. For example, entering =BORDER(TRUE,,,,) outlines the selected range. Entering =BORDER(,TRUE,TRUE,FALSE,FALSE,,) removes the top and bottom outline and adds the left and right.

265

CLEAR(value)

This command clears data like the Edit-Clear command. First select the cell or range that you want to clear (you can do this in the macro also), then use this command to clear the selected data. Or you can enter the type of information you want to clear in place of the value: entering 1 clears everything, 2 clears formats, 3 clears formulas and 4 clears notes.

CLOSE(logical)

This command is equivalent to the File-Close command. CLOSE removes the active window from the screen. Enter either TRUE or FALSE as the logical value. Entering TRUE saves the worksheet and closes it. Entering FALSE closes the worksheet without saving. Entering no value (using empty parentheses) brings up a dialog box asking if you want to save changes made.

COLUMN.WIDTH(width,reference)

This command sets the column width for any column like the Format-Column Width command. Enter the desired column width as the width argument and the column number as the reference argument. You'll have to convert the column letter into a value. The Options-Workspace-R1C1 command can be helpful for this. For example, entering =COLUMN.WIDTH(15,2) increases column B to 15 characters. It can be useful to stack several of these commands in a macro to adjust many columns at once.

266

COMBINATION(number)

This command sets a combination chart for the currently active chart. Enter the desired combination chart number (as shown in the options produced by the Gallery-Combination command).

COPY()
CANCEL.COPY()

The COPY command copies information in the currently selected cell or range. This is useful in preparation for pasting the information with the PASTE command. The CANCEL.COPY command removes the marquee after copying.

CUT()

Equivalent to the Edit-Cut command, CUT is useful for moving data from one location to another. The macro should select the data, issue the CUT command, then move to the new location and paste.

DATA.DELETE( )

This command is equivalent to the Data-Delete menu command. Use it to delete records according to the current criteria range.

DATA.FIND(logical)

This command finds a record in the database, or exits the find procedure. Enter TRUE to find records or FALSE to exit the find procedure.

DATA.FORM( )

This command brings up the database data form for the currently set database. Use it after defining the database and criteria ranges.

267

DISPLAY(formula,gridline,heading,zero,color)

This command displays or hides various elements on the worksheet. Enter TRUE in any argument that you want displayed or FALSE if you don't want it displayed. Enter a value from 1 to 8 for the color option to select a color for the worksheet. These arguments correspond to the check boxes on the Options-Display dialog box.

EXTRACT(logical)

The EXTRACT command extracts data from the active database according to the active criteria settings. Enter TRUE to extract unique records only or FALSE to extract all matching records.

FORMAT.FONT(name,size,bold,italic, underline,strike)

FORMAT.FONT(color,background,apply, name,size,bold,italic,underline,strike)

This command is equivalent to using the Format-Font menu command. It applies a font, size and style to the currently selected cell or range. There are two versions of this command. The first version should be used on normal worksheets and macro sheets. The second version should be used to manipulate the fonts on a chart.

Enter the name of the font in the name argument. Be sure to enter it with quotation marks. Enter TRUE or FALSE for any of the remaining arguments to turn them on or off. In the chart version, the color argument should be a value from 0 to 8 representing the color you want for the font. The value 0 tells Excel to select the color automatically. Background values can be any of the following:

1   Automatic

2   Transparent

3   White Out

The apply argument applies the font selection to all like elements in the chart. Enter TRUE or FALSE as the value of this argument.

FORMAT.NUMBER(format)

This command chooses a numeric format for the currently selected cell or range. Enter the number format as a text string, as in =FORMAT.NUMBER("#,##0.00"). Use any format from the list provided in the Format-Number command.

FORMULA.GOTO(reference)

This command performs the same function as the Formula-Goto menu option. Enter an address for the cell or range that you want to locate. You can also enter a range name, provided the name is already defined for a range.

GALLERY.AREA(number)
GALLERY.BAR(number)
GALLERY.COLUMN(number)
GALLERY.LINE(number)
GALLERY.PIE(number)
GALLERY.SCATTER(number)
PREFERRED( )

269

These commands are equivalent to the various Gallery options. They set the type of chart for the active chart. Enter the respective chart type number as the number. To see these numbers, use the corresponding menu command.

NEW(type)
NEW?( )

This command is equivalent to the File-New command. The type argument represents the type of worksheet to open. Enter 1 to create a worksheet, 2 to create a chart, or 3 to create a macro sheet. If you use the ? (question) mark after the command, Excel brings up the standard File-New dialog box where you can choose one of the three types of windows to create.

OPEN(name text)
OPEN?( )

This command is equivalent to the File-Open menu command. Enter the name of the file that you want to open in place of the name text argument. Make sure that you enter the name with quotation marks, as in OPEN("myfile"). Enter the entire directory path if the file is not in the default path, as in OPEN("C:\DATA\myfile").

PASTE()

The PASTE command pastes information from the clipboard into the worksheet at the pointer location. PASTE is useful after you use the COPY or CUT command.

PRINT?()

270

This command is equivalent to the File-Print command. When this command is encountered in a macro, Excel brings up the Print dialog box and waits for you to make your selections. This can be useful as the final command in a macro that performs many of the print setup operations for you and then prints the worksheet.

ROW.HEIGHT(height)

This command is equivalent to the Format-Row Height command. It sets the height of the active row in the worksheet. Enter the desired height in points (a point is 1/72 of an inch) as the height argument. Be sure to select the desired row first by simply moving the pointer to that row.

SET.CRITERIA
SET.DATABASE

These commands set the current criteria range and database range, like the Data-Set Criteria and Data-Set Database menu commands. Be sure to select the desired range before using these commands.

SET.PRINT.AREA()

This command activates the currently selected range as the current print area. It is equivalent to the Options-Set Print Area command. If only one cell is selected, the command removes the print area.

SET.PREFERRED()

This is equivalent to the Gallery-Set Preferred command, which sets the Preferred chart type to match the currently selected chart. Then, when you use the PREFERRED command (listed above), Excel duplicates the chart you set.

SET.PRINT.TITLES()

271

This command activates the currently selected range as the titles range for printouts. First, select the desired range of cells, then use this command as you would use the Options-Set Print Titles menu command.

Duplicating Keyboard and Mouse Actions

Excel provides a number of macro commands that duplicate actions you can take with the mouse or keyboard. This includes entering information into cells, selecting cells and so on. Following are explanations of the common commands and their arguments.

FORMULA(formula text,reference)

The FORMULA function enters data into a cell of the worksheet as if you had typed it yourself. This data can be a text string, a number or a formula. The formula text is the data you would like entered. Be sure to surround this data with quotation marks. Excel deciphers whether your entry is a number, formula or text string. Excel uses the same criteria for making this decision as it does when you type data from the keyboard. Anything beginning with an = sign is a formula. Anything beginning with an alphabetic character (except a range name) is a text string, and so on. The reference is the cell into which you want to enter the data. If the reference is omitted, Excel uses the current cell. If the cell receiving this data already contains information, Excel will replace the old data with your new entry.

MOVE(x position,y position)

272

This command moves a window to another screen location, as when you drag on its title bar. The x position and y position represent the horizontal and vertical positions of the upper-left corner of the window. The x and y positions are measured in points from the upper-left corner of the screen.

SELECT(selection)

The SELECT command is equivalent to selecting a cell or range. Simply enter the desired cell or range in the selection argument. The selection can be specified as a cell or range on the current worksheet, using the form !A5 or !A5:B6. You can also refer to a named range, as in !Sales.

Alternatively, you can make the selection relative to the currently active cell by making the argument an R1C1-style reference entered as a text string. For example, entering =SELECT("RC[3]") moves the pointer three columns to the right. Entering =SELECT("R[-3]C[2]") moves the pointer three rows up and two columns to the right.

SIZE(width,height)

This is equivalent to changing the size of a window with the mouse or command menu. Enter the desired width and height in points. Excel changes the lower-right corner of the active window to match your specifications.

Controlling Macro Operation

Excel includes a group of commands that control how macros operate. You'll find these commands useful for many of your macros.

ALERT(message,type)

This command brings up an alert box containing a message that you design. Enter any message for the box as the message argument. Specify the type of alert box by entering its numeric value as the type argument. Entering 1 creates a "caution" box, 2 creates a "note" box, 3 creates a "stop" box. These are simply three different styles of messages.

273

BEEP(value)

This command causes a beep to sound. Enter any number for the value argument to control the length of time the beep sounds.

RETURN( )

This command is used at the end of a macro to return operation to the macro's starting point.

Sample Macros

Enter the macro listed below to add an outline to the currently selected range:

```
OUTLINE
=BORDER(TRUE,FALSE,FALSE,FALSE,FALSE,FALSE)
=RETURN()
```

The following macro removes the gridlines and the scroll bars from the worksheet.

```
GRIDS
=DISPLAY(FALSE,FALSE,TRUE,TRUE,0)
=WORKSPACE(FALSE,,FALSE,FALSE,TRUE,TRUE,"/",FALSE,TRUE,3)
=RETURN()
```

274

As a good alternative to using the mouse to widen columns, you can enter the following macro that widens the current column by two characters each time you press the macro command.

```
WIDEN
=COLUMN.WIDTH(GET,CELL(16)+2)
=RETURN()
```

The following macro changes Font 3 to Roman, 14-point and then formats the currently selected range with the new Font 3.

```
ROMAN
=REPLACE.FONT(3,"Roman",14,FALSE,FALSE,FALSE,FALSE)
=FORMAT.FONT("Roman",14,FALSE,FALSE,FALSE,FALSE)
=RETURN()
```

To shrink the current window and move it to the bottom-right side of the screen, enter the following macro:

```
SHRINK
=SIZE(240,240)
=MOVE(250,80)
=RETURN()
```

276

277

278

279

280

281

284

285

287

288

Reader Feedback Card

Thank you for purchasing this book from Howard W. Sams & Company's FIRST BOOK series. Our intent with this series is to bring you timely, authoritative information that you can reference quickly and easily. You can help us by taking a minute to complete and return this card. We appreciate your comments and will use the information to better serve your needs.

1. Where did you purchase this book?

☐ Chain bookstore (Walden, B. Dalton) ☐ Direct mail
☐ Independent bookstore ☐ Book club
☐ Computer/Software store ☐ School bookstore
☐ Other _____
_____

2. Why did you choose this book? (Check as many as apply.)

☐ Price ☐ Appearance of book
☐ Author's reputation ☐ Howard W. Sam's reputation
☐ Quick and easy treatment of subject ☐ Only book available on subject

3. How do you use this book? (Check as many as apply.)

☐ As a supplement to the product manual ☐ As a reference
☐ In place of the product manual ☐ At home
☐ For self-instruction ☐ At work

4. Please rate this book in the categories below. G = Good; N = Needs improvement; U = Category is unimportant.

☐ Price ☐ Appearance
☐ Amount of information ☐ Accuracy
☐ Examples ☐ Quick Steps
☐ Inside cover reference ☐ Second color
☐ Table of contents ☐ Index
☐ Tips and cautions ☐ Illustrations
☐ Length of book
☐ How can we improve this book? _____

5. How many computer books do you normally buy in a year?

☐ 1–5 ☐ 5–10 ☐ More than 10
☐ I rarely purchase more than one book on a subject.
☐ I may purchase a beginning and an advanced book on the same subject.
☐ I may purchase several books on particular subjects.
(such as _____)

6. Have you purchased other Howard W. Sams or Hayden books in the past year? ____
If yes, how many? _____

7. Would you purchase another book in the FIRST BOOK series? _____

8. What are your primary areas of interest in business software?
- ☐ Word processing (particularly _____)
- ☐ Spreadsheet (particularly _____)
- ☐ Database (particularly _____)
- ☐ Graphics (particularly _____)
- ☐ Personal finance/accounting (particularly _____)
- ☐ Other (please specify _____)

Other comments on this book or the Howard W. Sams book line: _____
_____

Name _____
Company _____
Address _____
City _____ State _____ Zip _____
Daytime telephone number _____
Title of this book _____

Fold here